LEADING SCHOOLS IN THE 21ST CENTURY

HEADS

ESSAYS IN LEADERSHIP FOR CHANGING TIMES

Edited by
Brenda Despontin and Nigel Richardson

Published for the Girls' Schools Association and
the Headmasters' and Headmistresses' Conference
by John Catt Educational Ltd
2007

First Published 2007

by John Catt Educational Ltd,
Great Glemham, Saxmundham, Suffolk IP17 2DH
Tel: 01728 663666 Fax: 01728 663415
E-mail: enquiries@johncatt.co.uk
Website: www.johncatt.com

ISBN: 978 1 904724 49 0

Set and designed by
John Catt Educational Limited

Printed and bound in Great Britain
by Bell & Bain, Glasgow, Scotland

CONTENTS

About the Contributors

Dr Priscilla Chadwick has been Principal of Berkhamsted Collegiate School since 1996. She studied Theology at Cambridge, her PGCE at Oxford, and an MA in Curriculum Studies and later a PhD in Education at the University of London. Her teaching career includes being Head of Religious Education departments in both the independent and state sectors, serving as a state school Deputy and Head in comprehensive schools in London, and being Dean of Educational Development at South Bank University. She was Chairman of HMC in 2005.

Keith Dawson retired as Headmaster of Haberdashers' Aske's School, Elstree, in 1996, having previously held posts in both the maintained and independent sectors. Since then he has led school inspections for HMC and ISI. He has been involved with appraisal since the 1970s, and since 1996 he has appraised many Heads and Deputies of HMC, GSA and IAPS schools. He has been a governor of a number of independent and state schools and he is currently on the boards of Bristol Grammar and Exeter schools.

Dr Brenda Despontin has been Headmistress of Haberdashers' Monmouth School for Girls since 1997. She has a first degree in psychology, a masters' in Thomas Hardy, a doctorate in children's literature and an MBA on educational leadership. After teaching at The British School in Brussels and working as a residential supervisor in a home for disturbed teenage girls, she went on to teach at comprehensive and independent schools before setting up the girls' division at the King's School, Macclesfield. She was President of GSA in 2006.

Gill Dixon became Head of Trent College in 2006. She holds an honours degree and PGCE in Mathematics from Warwick University and also took a MBA in Educational Management at Leicester. After teaching in schools and university in Zimbabwe, Gill taught maths, was Housemistress and Officer in Charge of the CCF at Oakham, drawing upon her expertise as a Squadron Leader in the Royal Air Force. She then moved to Cheadle Hulme School as Deputy Head, where her responsibilities included strategic planning and development, curriculum development, staffing and disciplinary issues, assessment, recording and value-added systems.

Sarah Evans has been Head of King Edward VI High School for Girls since 1996. Before that she was Head of Friends School, Saffron Walden. She has served on the education committees of both SHMIS and GSA/HMC. She has been a governor of four schools and is involved in a number of partnerships with the state sector. She is a trustee of a national out-of-hours learning trust and runs courses for those returning to teaching after career breaks.

Clarissa Farr was appointed High Mistress of St Paul's Girls' School in 2006, having previously been Principal of Queenswood for ten years. Before that, she taught in a sixth form college, a large Bristol comprehensive and a city grammar school, as well as spending a period teaching overseas in Hong Kong. She was Chairman of the Boarding Schools' Association from 2001-2002 and President of the Girls' Schools Association in 2005.

Marion Gibbs is Headmistress of James Allen's Girls' School, London. She was previously HMI (Schools) and an OFSTED RgI, and is a long-serving ISI Reporting Inspector. She has taught in a variety of maintained and independent schools, in two prisons and for the Open University. She is passionate about Classics, was a Chief Examiner, and has published a book on Greek Tragedy, as well as contributing chapters to educational books and writing a regular column.

Dr Tim Hands studied the violin at the Guildhall School of Music before reading English at King's College London and then Oxford. He was briefly a stipendiary Lecturer at Oriel College, then a housemaster at King's School, Canterbury, Second Master at Whitgift, and Head of The Portsmouth Grammar School. In 2008 he becomes Master of Magdalen College School. His family has a long interest in teaching: his father left the independent sector in the 1960s to become Head of one of the country's largest comprehensive schools, and an ancestor was Schoolmaster on the *Victory* in Napoleonic times. He has written four books about Victorian literature.

Dr David Hempsall retired after 12 years as Head of QEGS, Blackburn, in 2007. He was educated at the Manchester Grammar School and Sidney Sussex College, Cambridge, where he read History. His doctorate from the University of Kent followed research into aspects of the French Reformation. He spent ten years as Head at Scarborough College from 1985-95. He is a former Treasurer of HMC, and has served on ISC's Governing Council, its Finance and General Purposes Committee and the ISI Committee.

Pat Langham has been Head of Wakefield Girls' High School since 1987. She was educated at Carlisle and County High School for Girls. She studied English and Russian at Leeds University and Leningrad Polytechnic, obtaining a BA Hons Degree followed by her PGCE. In 1987 she obtained her Master of Education degree. Her first three posts were in state co-educational comprehensives, the last one as the Pastoral Deputy in a school of 1300. She became Principal of Wakefield Grammar School Foundation in September 2000, and is President of the Girls' Schools Association in 2007.

Tony Little has been Head Master of Eton College since 2002. He taught at Tonbridge and Brentwood, where he was Head of English and Drama and a boarding house master before becoming Headmaster of Chigwell School and then Oakham School. He took up his post at Eton 30 years after leaving there as a schoolboy with sights set firmly on a life in anything but teaching.

Hilary Moriarty is National Director of the Boarding Schools' Association. She is an ex-grammar school girl, graduate of Trinity College, Dublin, and Leicester University. She trained in tertiary education and has worked in colleges of further education, grammar and comprehensive schools. Thirteen years of her career have been spent as Deputy Head at Red Maids' School in Bristol, during its boarding school days, and as Headmistress of Bedgebury, a girls' day and boarding school in Kent which closed in 2006.

Dr Nigel Richardson is Head of the Perse School, Cambridge, having been Second Master at Uppingham, Head of the Dragon School, Oxford, and Deputy Head of the King's School, Macclesfield. He is an independent school governor, and was editor of the HMC magazine *Conference & Common Room* from 1999-2002. He has written history books for children and training literature for the Industrial Society, and contributes regularly to the educational press. He was Chairman of HMC in 2007.

Dr Martin Stephen has been High Master of St Paul's School since 2004. In his earlier career he taught at Uppingham, was a housemaster at Haileybury, Second Master at Sedbergh, Headmaster of the Perse School, Cambridge, and High Master of Manchester Grammar School. He is the author of 17 academic titles on poetry and naval history, of four acclaimed novels in the 'Henry Gresham' sequence of historical crime thrillers, and is a prolific press writer.

Dr Bernard Trafford has been Head of Wolverhampton Grammar School since 1990 and becomes Headmaster of the Royal Grammar School, Newcastle upon Tyne, in 2008. During the 1990s he carried out doctoral research into democratic school management styles and the development of what is now known as 'student voice', and that experience stimulated him to become busy writing and speaking in those and analogous areas. In 2006 he edited the HMC/John Catt Educational book i^2= *independent and innovative: examples of innovation in HMC schools*. He is Chairman of HMC in 2007-8.

Vicky Tuck became Principal of Cheltenham Ladies' College in 1996. She was previously Deputy Head at City of London School for Girls. Prior to that, positions held include PGCE Course Director at London's Institute of Education; Head of Modern Languages at Bromley High; and teacher of French and Italian at Putney High School. She is President of GSA in 2008.

Introduction

The Role of the Head

by Brenda Despontin

"Do it your way." That was it. Newly appointed to Headship for the following autumn, and part of a spring inspection team, I had summoned the courage to ask advice of another team member, the recently retired Head of a prestigious school. What did he think any new Head should remember above all else?

"It's simple, Brenda. Do it your way."

A book which aims to reflect modern Headship in a helpful, honest manner had to let its contributors do it their way too. This complex role demands so much of us as individuals, and demands so much of our individuality, that any attempt to conform to a prescribed 'type' is doomed from the start.

So the chapters ahead do not conform to a given format, either: they are rich in anecdote and ripe in both personal recommendations and wise counsel, some of it born inevitably of painful errors of judgement along the way. The Heads write with honesty, humour and insight. Above all, the contributors are reassuring in their unfailing passion for what they do, and (though much has changed since a similar collection of essays entitled *Head to Head* was published some years ago), what remains as a constant and unassailable fact is that we love what we do.

Hopefully, that passion and delight, which permeates all the chapters here, will inspire colleagues to think seriously about the move to the Head's desk at a time when the importance of succession planning for Headship has never been greater. There is a recruitment crisis in the maintained sector resulting in thousands of posts being re-advertised each year, with the National College of School Leadership now tasked to explore the feasibility of alternative models, including headship of a federation of schools, and school leaders from outside education. In the independent sector, applications for posts are fewer than in the past, and a cross-Association leadership initiative is under consideration to train and secure our future school leaders.

We know why this has happened, of course. When Churchill claimed 70 years ago that Headmasters had "powers at their disposal with which Prime Ministers had never yet been invested" the world was a very different place. Many Heads still hankered then after the autonomy and the cultivated mystique of a Thomas Arnold or a Miss Beale. The model of Headship was autocratic and the Head's personal qualities focused chiefly on scholarship.

That past is most definitely a different country, and Headteachers today are expected to solve all manner of social ills, from obesity to text bullying. We juggle finances to achieve the impossible and inhabit a culture obsessed with testing and assessment. Accountability can make cowards of us all as we wrestle with the demonic demographics, with league tables, with unreasonable or poorly-trained governors, with arrogant parents and with an often immoral press hungry for a spicy story from what they see as nothing more than schools for toffs.

When we're not sitting somewhere having what our governors call our 'vision' we're running a complex business, the end product of which is nebulous to quantify. We are managers of personnel, marketing, budgets, health and safety, employment and recruitment – and the curriculum, of course. We must have available all data and details when asked, be Relate counsellors for warring parents, mediate in petty staff disputes, prepare meaningful assemblies, never expect thanks – but, never, ever, forget to thank everyone ourselves.

And still we love what we do.

In such a context it is hardly surprising, however, that a growing number of good senior staff in our schools now hesitate before scrabbling to the ladder's top rung. They have read the stories of 'superheads' in both sectors sacked for failing to deliver: they have seen the often quite public breakdown of a few who have tried heroically to make a difference somewhere. They prefer to play safe.

The changing structure of school management has forged a two-edged sword. Distributed leadership facilitates personal development of aspiring, talented colleagues giving them significant whole-school responsibility, and a chance to implement and manage change, but it often brings simultaneously a sense of fulfilment and a job satisfaction which occasionally works against any hunger for further promotion. The structures for training colleagues in leadership skills are better than ever in our schools, but we can ill afford to ignore the desperate need for us to nurture Headship itself. Membership of a leadership team should be considered a means to an end, not an end in itself.

Writing about leadership 15 years ago, Senge[1] reminded us that a learning organisation is one that is 'continually expanding its capacity to create its future', and independent schools must be proactive and imaginative now in their strategies for succession planning. Who would disagree with John Dunford's claim that 'Nothing could be more important for schools than to ensure the next generation of Headteachers'?

The reality is that by 2009, 30% of Heads currently serving in state schools will have retired, and 85% of Heads are over 45. Yet in a recent survey conducted by the Institute of Policy Studies for the General Teaching Council, only 2.5% of secondary teachers were considering Headship as a goal, leading the Institute's Director to accuse the government of 'culpable neglect'.

So the collection of essays which follows aims to celebrate and recommend Headship. Enthusiastic practitioners, some new and some very experienced, demystify their daily routines and suggest ways in which even the trickiest situation can be tackled successfully. For new Heads it will be an invaluable collection, both in its reassurance and inspiration, particularly in the chapters by Gill Dixon and Clarissa Farr. But the collection holds gifts for us all.

Despite the cynicism that (justifiably) greeted much 90s 'management speak' in education, the recommendation to call the Head the 'lead learner' (which mercifully never quite took off) did make some sense to me. Has there been a day at your desk when you did not learn something?

That is why I find it so hard to respond when well-meaning friends say: "After ten years in post, it must surely be a lot easier now".

Because we are bombarded with new directives, because we have to live simultaneously in the past, present and future, and because we interact daily with hundreds of complex people, we cannot ever stop learning, and I found myself jotting down some excellent ideas as I proof-read the chapters, asking myself why *I* had never thought of handling things in that particular way. For our colleagues' contributions to this, the first of a series on Leading Schools today, Nigel Richardson and I are deeply grateful, knowing only too well how such a request would have added to the demands of each Head's intray.

Sergiovanni[2] described Leadership as a 'quest ... not a given … not an answer, not a fixed destination'. The authors of these chapters confirm that we can only beat the path to successful Headship by walking it, with each day, each year, each challenge, each change providing a constant voyage of discovery for the privileged traveller.

The pages which follow also hold moments all Heads will recognise, from those staffroom power bases who promote the 'hidden curriculum' described in Sarah Evans' essay, to David Hempsall's pertinent comments on Heads and bursars, with his excellent suggestion on how to spend any money left from a previous budget! Nigel Richardson reflects on the often problematic relationship with governors, and Vicky Tuck comments on our ability to juggle demands and manage our time.

Martin Stephen provides wise advice on marketing, Priscilla Chadwick assesses the merits and pitfalls of Development projects, and Tony Little offers anecdotes and guidance on PR. He declares that we should tell our story bravely, unafraid as Heads to speak out publicly on matters which are important to young people. Marion Gibbs reminds us of the importance of looking after ourselves and of keeping a life beyond the desk, and Keith Dawson kindly agreed to contribute a section on appraisal, having carried out the exercise for each of this book's editors (and for many other Heads, too) over the years.

Some readers will hold different views from those expressed here: not every boarding school Head functions as Hilary Moriarty describes, though some do. Not every school has its medical centre as a 'clearing house of pastoral problems', but Tim Hands does – and it clearly works well for him.

There is no *one size fits all* model to Headship, as I was reminded all those years ago. How could there be, given the diverse nature of our schools? It is that rich diversity within each day which gives us so much pleasure as Heads. It is a rich diversity of independent educational provision which we promote in our associations. Our leadership style is part of that celebration of individuality.

It seems fitting to conclude my introduction with an anecdote from a former Headmaster. Peter Attenborough is well known to both editors, and he recalls fondly an occasion very early in his long and distinguished career when he was summoned to his Headmaster's study. On the desk between them was a large tome, on the cover of which, emblazoned boldly, were the letters 'H.T.R.T.S.'. Noticing Peter's puzzled gaze, the Head said: "I expect you are wondering what I keep in there. Well, that's where I store all those memos and letters from staff, parents and governors who try to tell me 'How To Run The School'.

This book is not intended for that file, and it makes no claim to provide a definitive guide to Headship. But it is our hope that its content will encourage those contemplating Headship to go ahead. Equally we hope that it will reassure those already in post, confirming what most of us believe, that we change lives by what we do, and that we are privileged to be engaged in the most fascinating, worthwhile and important of jobs.

Whether you are that Head sitting at your fireplace with a labrador at your feet, as depicted in Pat Langham's chapter, or whether you are busy modelling yourself on Tim Hands' woodcut by Wynkyn de Worde, there *is* only one way to be a Head, and that is your way.

[1]Senge, P: *The Fifth Discipline* (1990).
[2]Sergiovanni, T J: *Leadership: What's in it for our schools?* (2001).

Chapter 1

The First Hundred Days

Gill Dixon

This is adapted from a talk given on the HMC New Heads' course at Cumberland Lodge, Windsor, at Easter 2007.

It is a delight to be here, one year on… Unlike the great and the good (and the proven) who have spoken before me this weekend, here I am, only 30 weeks old. I have no great wisdom nor experience to share, simply a few minutes in which to tell my story. A story, full of emotion, adrenalin, successes, failures, humour, real fear and deep, deep joy. Rather than ramble aimlessly, I have sectioned my story into six chapters: the first day, the first relationships, the first routines, the first lessons, the first plans and the first emotions.

The first day. The build up to my very first day and that very first staff meeting was, for me, one of the most nerve-wracking, worrying and most difficult of times. The need for me to make a good first impression was paramount, overwhelming. I wanted to appear calm, confident, experienced, poised. I wanted to ooze gravitas. But where does gravitas come from? I even considered tying my hair up in a bun, wearing a tweed suit and a set of pearls because I thought that I might look more the part. I didn't. The worries over that first day grew, throughout the last weeks of August, to become quite a monster.

Change, moving to a new place, always awakens the senses and I have very vivid memories of that first day, even the smells, the colours. I remember sitting on my own, feeling cold, at the front of the chapel at the beginning of the staff meeting with 100 teaching staff silently filing in and sitting on the back rows. I remember all their eyes on me and that there seemed to be so many of them. I felt very young and very vulnerable. I remember the nervous flutters deep in the stomach and the thoughts running through my head: 'Will I be able to pull it off or will they find me out? Will they be able to see that I am not really a Head but that I am in fact just a deputy who managed to get through the interview?'

I remember fluffing my well-rehearsed opening line. Then I took a deep breath and eventually clicked into gear. I was warm and inspiring and energising and positive, and I was well-prepared and said exactly the right things. The staff gave me a lovely reception. I guarantee that it will be the same for you. Your staff will want you to be good because everyone wants to be part of a good school. They will not want you to fail. Everyone will be on your side. It is a lovely audience to play to, a very easy gig … and not at all the monster that I had imagined it to be.

At the end, I felt fabulous: I actually felt a bit different, changed. I certainly felt that I had grown a couple of inches, though that didn't last long. As colleagues rushed off to departmental meetings, I walked back to my rather grand office and sat behind the huge leather desk on my throne to realise that my feet didn't actually reach the ground. Back down to earth then!

Then I thought: 'Well, what do I do now?' There was nothing on my huge desk. I considered curtain-making for a brief moment, and then managed to find some old files in a drawer and just spread them around a bit so I could pretend I was doing something important.

The first assembly was, for me, another magical moment. My vivid memory is of standing at the back of the hall, staring at the back of the heads of my 780 pupils and thinking how smart and shiny they looked. Then, flanked by my robed senior prefects, being processed down the aisle … and you could have heard a pin drop. As I stood at the lectern and sensed the size and the responsibility of my new job, I felt very humbled and quite emotional. One of the biggest differences I have found between being a Head and a deputy is emotion. For me, being a deputy meant working hard, learning as much as I could, doing a good job, pleasing my boss. But being a Head is much more emotional. For me, it means loving my school.

On my very first day here, as I was strolling around, trying to work out where everything was, I thought to ask our estates manager to give me the alternative tour of Trent. We walked and walked and walked through all the nooks and crannies. He showed me the underground cellars (where the Common Room used to keep their wine), the well underneath the main building which had been sealed off for decades, the beauty spots, the grot spots (yes, there are a couple).

I then asked if I could climb up the clock tower and sit on top of the school. He gave me a bit of a funny look but eventually agreed, though he warned me that it was rather a dodgy climb and no one had done it in a long time. So, on with the trainers and off we set climbing up through the Shuker House roof space, up very shaky ladders, crossing steaming hot water pipes, clambering over bells which hadn't rung for many years, until eventually we arrived at a tiny hatch which led up on the roof. Out we popped and nervously we hopped up the steep incline of the slate roof for me to sit on top of this school, Trent College. It is a fantastic sight, this beautiful school with such a wonderful campus, and I can honestly tell you that I fell in love with Trent just at that moment.

The first relationships. Most staff will be incredibly nervous when they first meet you. It is a very strange feeling, which I still cannot get used to. This title that I carry has such a power and a presence and an influence, even though inside it is just little ol' me. In my first week, one staff member – desperate to give that good first impression as he walked alongside me and burbling through some nervous conversation – walked into a tree. I lost another who slid down a grassy bank mid-flow. People stumbling over their words, hands shaking, beads of sweat, flushed faces: the reaction just to meeting me. I shall never get used to it!

Another unusual animal that you will encounter as a Head is the sycophant. I have found it very difficult to separate the sycophants in the Common Room from those staff who genuinely do agree with and support me. Thirty weeks in, and everyone still tells me that I am fabulous, that they agree with all that I am doing and planning to do. So far, it is proving difficult to find an honest critic, even amongst my own SMT or governors – or perhaps, I am indeed fabulous? No. I mustn't begin to believe in myself at all! (You can see how it happens though.)

The relationship with my Chairman is critical and I am very fortunate to have an outstanding and talented one. Though I do not have very much contact with him, perhaps only once a fortnight, he is always there and very ready to offer support and wisdom. He loves his school, he is very perceptive and he knows the difference between governance and management. His style is very much to stand back and let me get on with it.

As a Head I have finally understood now what it is that governors do. I never quite got it as a deputy. I have worked hard to develop individual relationships with the majority of the board already, even going to visit them in their own workplaces and being as interested in them as they are in Trent. I feel comfortable with them now, and each one does something to help me directly. They give me advice; they help me interview key staff members; they sort out pressures to do with money and litigation; they have brilliant ideas about how to make the business side of things work – and they are helping me build our buildings. I have learned so much business, legal and techno-speak, just by standing alongside them. It is a real relief to be able to delegate some stuff upwards.

I also have a rather unique and fabulous bursar. He is fully involved in our school life; he goes on school trips; he listens to the younger children read each week; he buys the odd keg of beer for the staff bar; and also he is as hard as nails. An endearing and very effective skills-set! We meet little and often, and we share everything together.

My PA retires next month and I know that it will be very difficult to find as good a replacement. I have never had one before and it is taking me a long time to learn how to use a PA fully. I have always been used to doing my own admin, to a high standard and very quickly. I know that I need to change these habits and to be able to let go of more to her. We have that lovely relationship which is professional when it needs to be, but is also informal and full of humour when it needs to be. Regular pranks in the office balance our sanity.

The SMT that I inherited is unusually big: 12 staff, but I chose to continue with it and evolve it as and when appropriate. Their routine had always been to have an SMT meeting each week on Friday, starting at 2pm and often going on for four hours. The agendas were packed full of lots of little bits of business (the tactical stuff) and there was little time to debate the big issues (the strategic stuff).

I changed this pattern immediately after I arrived. I meet with each of my SMT separately for one hour, either weekly or fortnightly, to clear away the little bits of business (the reactive and operational stuff). SMT meetings are now timetabled in for one hour on a Tuesday morning, with agendas only one or two items long – and always to do with planning, looking ahead and strategy. We have an informal meeting once a month for good ideas and a chat. I have also started to pass out regular reading material a couple of times each term. There are some remarkably good things coming out from the National College for School Leadership.

My relationships with the staff are very good. I have also begun to break down some of the barriers which have existed between teaching and support staff and there are regular get-togethers at School House for all to come and share a glass of wine. I have an open door policy and encourage staff to drop in early morning or late afternoon, even if they just want to say "hello". I spend my break time in the Common Room, but I do not go in at lunch time so that they can have a moan about me if they want to.

We have a briefing for all staff once a week. I carefully script my staff briefings so that I get the priorities right and don't miss anything, or anyone out. I am careful to say "we" and "us" rather than "I" and "you". I really believe in praising in public and reprimanding in private, so I always make sure that briefings to the whole staff are upbeat and positive. Most mornings, I take time to write cards to staff, with carefully written messages in them to recognise and acknowledge those who have done that bit more. I do this only because, throughout my career, I have always kept and cherished those that were written to me by my Head.

In my first term, I learned the names of about 100 pupils quite naturally, easily, in a school of 780, and then I found that I wasn't learning any more. So now, I have little photos on slips of paper that I study when I have a spare ten minutes and am trying to add a couple each day. I am up to about 160 now. It makes a huge difference!

The first routines. My commute to work is 320 paces – what a pleasure! I am at my desk at 8am, meeting with my two deputies for 20 minutes before school starts to update each other and to connect everything together. One of the highlights of my day is chapel each morning where, for 20 minutes I can collect my private thoughts and strength for the day. It starts off my day in the right way; thoughtful, hopeful, pupil-centred.

About half of my week is taken up with regular fixed meetings with each of my SMT. The other half of my diary is variable, though invariably it is absolutely full. On some days I am so busy that I can't see past the next couple of hours, and I don't know quite what to expect or to plan for.

The step up from deputy to Head is much bigger that I expected. As a deputy, there were always moments in the day when I could drift into some low-level routine and hide behind some simple therapeutic administrative task. As a Head that never really happens. The day is packed full and hugely varied, as it was as a deputy, but the difference is every part of the day, every task that you are required to carry out, is of 'high order'. You cannot lose yourself in some timetabling conundrum or in doing a bit of photocopying.

I have also really learnt the true meaning of the word resilience. I always quoted it in my letters of application and very much thought it a characteristic of mine, with my marathon running and sporting interests. But I have now understood that resilience for a Head is not so much about your physical strength and stamina; it is about emotional strength and stamina. Everyone you meet through the day, everyone who comes into your office through the day will want something from you: advice, encouragement, solutions, a better job, their ego stroked, money, or they will have come just to offload their worries and stresses on you. I think that it is a little like a doctor's surgery. By the end of the day I have often given out so much that I feel absolutely drained, sucked dry, empty … and yet that is when resilience is absolutely necessary. I have to stand up tall, put a big smile on my face and be that 'oasis of calm and reservoir of hope' that all schools need.

I have reminded myself periodically that I must never show it if I am tired. If I am tired, the SMT will be tired – and if the SMT is tired, the school will be too. If I am worried about something, I will not reveal it, and thus pass on my worries to those who cannot help. I am naturally very energetic and optimistic – and I am now beginning to see the impact of my own character being reflected back at me by my school. I've always been inclined to see the best in people and to trust them to get on with it: I do not micro-manage. I hope this encourages my deputies and senior managers.

I eat alongside my pupils most days, and though they weren't at all sure of what to make of it in the early days, now they do not mind me joining them and chatting. I try to get home around 6pm to play with my children and get them into bed for 7.30pm. Most weeks I am required to attend evening functions for three or four nights a week. I am the first in the bar at 6pm on Friday to buy everyone a drink, but I don't stay too long because staff still stand a little to attention until I have gone, which is when they really let their hair down.

The first lessons. Some very simple lessons that I quickly learnt in the first few weeks:

I have learnt that what works in one school doesn't necessarily transfer to another.

I have seen that what can seemingly be a really big concern in one school, demanding lots of resource and energy, can in another school be very straightforward and simple.

I have seen the importance of spotting the quick fixes and just doing them straight away.

I have learnt not to say "yes" in the corridor.

I have learnt not say: "Well at Oakham we did this and at Cheadle Hulme we did that…"

I have learnt not to promise what I can't deliver.

I have learnt that what I thought would be the most difficult decisions to make – expulsions, staff disciplinary hearings *etc* – are actually not that difficult to make. Deep down inside, I know the decision is right, even if there are people who do not agree with me. I can feel that it is right, if it is right for my school.

I am learning to grow a pretty thick skin and not to take any criticisms personally.

I have learnt not to worry too much about any future problems, and what could, or would, happen by just dealing with the current issues. Somehow that way, the future ones never seem to come up in the end.

I am also now beginning to learn that I can't keep using the excuse: 'Well I'm just the new girl'!

The first plans. My initial aims for the first term (the first year, in fact), were modest. I wasn't going to change anything. My plan was to secure my staff and pupils, and then just to sit back, and watch and listen and learn.

Thirty weeks later we have, as a school, focused and expressed our core values, and we are in the midst of re-branding the school. We have begun considering curriculum developments, and we have implemented a new system of classroom management and rewards and sanction structures. We are looking to improve our uniform, have re-introduced whole school assemblies and exeats, have got the bells in the clock tower ringing again for the first time in 12 years, have found and sung the Trent Hymn for the first time in 30 years, are establishing a Foundation for the school, have re-introduced staff supervision, have clarified the school rules, and have drawn up plans for a new library, dining hall and an expansion to our junior school.

One of the biggest challenges I have faced is in judging the pace of change. I am sure that I have probably set off too many hares, but so far it all seems to be holding together quite well. I also see that the pace of change at my school has been a little dictated by what went before.

We are also in the process of establishing an Improvement Plan. This has been an interesting process, which I have been through a couple of times before in other schools. I have found that Development Plans too often become just bits of paper that most staff, parents and pupils are not really aware of. In order to maintain a focus and a profile for our plan, we have determined four clear Strategic Intents, which we are to achieve over the next two years. We talk about these Intents a lot in briefings and meetings, almost developing them into mantras, and so that the language is picked up and echoed by our staff and pupils.

Our strategic intents are:

1. To create a success and high-achievement culture throughout the whole school.

2. To develop a stronger and more cohesive community.

3. To provide a broad and a balanced 'total curriculum' throughout the whole school and so give our students the best possible preparation for their future lives.

4. To secure the future development and ambitions of Trent College and its junior school.

I have found communication to be one of the biggest challenges of my job. I am quite good at delegating and I believe in the principle that, as a Head, you should only do what only you can do. But I am also increasingly convinced that a Head should never delegate communication. It is much more powerful for me, to stand up and speak directly to parents, staff and pupils, rather than try to deliver my message using a notice board or through my deputy. It is up to me to articulate the message, and for the vision to have the impact. And I know if I don't articulate it, I will never know how I am being perceived.

Writing speeches and public speaking is a huge part of the job. As a mathematician to my core, I have had to work really hard to develop what are, for me, unnatural skills. But, as in all things, there is no magic here other than the usual practice and preparation. I find that I quite like public speaking now, and I am certainly finding that I am becoming more comfortable, more confident and sometimes even unscripted.

The first emotions. Fear! The job of Head is made up of so many different parts: the pupils, the staff, the academic, the pastoral, finance, the junior school, the curriculum, governance, parents, marketing, alumni and development, registrar and admissions, the community. As a deputy I felt reasonably skilled in about a third of these areas, and the others I am working very hard to learn. When I look at each of these aspects separately, each seems very finite and achievable. The moments of real fear have been, for me, those moments where for a fleeting second I see all of the different aspects of the job at once.

There have been several occasions over my two terms when I have felt frightened and overwhelmed by the demands on me; when, within a couple of hours, I have had to produce a financial report for governors, to give a presentation to parents, when I have an angry dad on the phone and an assembly for the sixth form to write, when a disciplinary has just happened and a concern with a member of staff has surfaced, whilst all the time I have four or five letters to respond to, and half a dozen phone calls to make.

But so far I have always managed to sit myself down with a cup of tea and to begin by doing one thing at a time. In the end I know, always, that I will manage. Fortunately, I am the sort of person who actually enjoys that bit of fear and adrenalin and pressure because it makes me feel alive. Moreover, I am also fortunate to be the sort of person who can put things down in the evening and sleep like a log every night. I am sure that you can't do this job if you are a worrier!

Loneliness. While I have developed some strong relationships with staff at school, deep down I am their employer – and that *does* make a difference. There is a gap between me and the rest of my school. The role of Head is such a massive one and there are moments when I have really felt the weight of the role and responsibility – for example when giving my judgement at the end of a disciplinary hearing to expel a pupil, or deciding on a bursary offer, or picking up the pieces of a broken family, or in dealing with bereavement, or in trying to encourage an exhausted colleague.

Work-life balance? No, I will be absolutely honest, and say that. I haven't found it yet; indeed, I am nowhere near doing so. My husband and I looked at each other at the beginning of the year, and we both recognised that we probably wouldn't be able to find *any* balance for a while. I think there are some times in your career when you have to just put your head down and get on with it. To make our family life work, my husband has taken a year out to look after our two young children, aged three and four, and actually he loves it.

On a typical day I am out from 8am until 6pm, with functions or commitments on most evenings each week. Weeks roll into weekends with commitments running throughout. If I find that I have got a spare half hour mid-week, I now take advantage of a break, though I still feel a little bit guilty that I am doing so while the rest of my school is at work. But I recognise the importance of finding the right balance between home and work, and I do see that this balance will not find itself. I know that it is up to me to make this happen.

Joy. I am convinced that being a Head is the busiest, the most difficult, the most adrenalin-filled, the most emotional, the most varied – and the best job in the world. So often, I have been overwhelmed and humbled by the qualities I have seen in my staff and students. It is a real privilege to lead a school and to have such a chance to influence and to make a difference. I am not sure that the role of Head will ever feel natural, or that I will ever feel that I can come close to filling it, but I wouldn't change my life for the world. I hope that your first hundred days are as thrilling as mine!

Chapter 2

Early Stages

Clarissa Farr

Becoming the Head of a school – whether for the first or second time – is rather like boarding a moving train. You haul yourself and your luggage into one of the rear carriages, slam the door hard and sit down heavily on your suitcase. (This is Day One.) In the succeeding days and weeks, you must gradually make your way towards the driver's cabin, not so quickly that you lose your balance and cause well-settled passengers in first class to spill their coffee, but yet not so slowly that the train threatens to run out of control or flick onto the wrong rails at the next set of points. Once you reach the driver's seat and can see through the windscreen where the train is going, you can view the way ahead and begin to consider the route. At about this point – in the distance – a sign looms up: 'End of Year One'.

As will be immediately obvious, I know very little about trains (despite having revisited *Thomas the Tank Engine* relatively recently) but this analogy does convey something of the headlong, forward-focused feeling that characterises the first year of Headship. You have joined a complex, moving, growing entity which has a life and momentum already in full flow: it takes time to understand it, recognise the bits that are spinning to perfection and find the bits that are spiky and rusty and need attention, but on which you might cut your fingers and most exciting of all, see clearly what lies ahead and where you want to go. Probably the most important thing during this year is to watch, listen and be patient: if you rush in with sudden change, you may risk a partial derailment.

My own experience in first Headship was particular in that I was appointed internally. This was both good and bad: good in that I already knew everyone and the systems were familiar so my initial learning curve was less steep; bad in that I had inevitably to withdraw somewhat from closer relationships with staff who had become my friends and find my way into a new relationship with everyone: staff, students and parents. When you come fresh to a school, you also have the advantage of seeing things clearly and objectively (for a time) which helps you identify where change is needed. The 'home-grown' Head, on the other hand, may be more risk-averse and slower to see what needs to be done.

Then of course there is one's predecessor. I have been extremely fortunate in taking over from two Heads (Audrey Butler at Queenswood in 1996 and Elizabeth Diggory at SPGS in 2006) who were both very happy to be handing over 'their' schools and who made the transition as smooth as they possibly could for me. Nevertheless, it can take time for the community to accept a new leader and you may even be seen by some as an unwelcome interloper, threatening to upset the happy equilibrium. Both my predecessors were also well known nationally and I can vividly recall the oft-repeated conference conversation:

A N Other delegate: "Hello! Which school are you from?"

Self: "Queenswood, actually."

A N Other delegate: "Oh, Queenswood! That's Audrey Butler's school isn't it?"

This went on for about five years. In school, too, for a long time, I worked in 'Mrs Butler's office' and lived in 'Mrs Butler's house', made coffee in 'Mrs Butler's kitchen' and hung out my washing in 'Mrs Butler's garden'. Again – be patient. You are now the Head and in time, people will accept you.

As I am perhaps beginning to imply, the fundamental requirement for being any kind of success as a Head is to build good relationships from the beginning. You can produce all the ambitious building projects and curriculum innovations and development plans you like, but unless these grow out of professional relationships that are based on trust and mutual respect, they will founder – or at best be short lived. This is not to say you must court popularity or be a push-over: indeed, you may well have to be tough (and I will come to toughness later) but you must work first for the kind of strength that will take you and your leadership team, together, through difficult situations.

As a new Head in first Headship, a most crucial relationship will be with the bursar. If, like me, you came into your role from deputy headship, you may have worked with a bursar before, but this partnership is essentially a new one. The caricature of the bursar as the person who says "No" to every exciting idea you have and whose sole mission is to punish teachers for spending half the year on holiday while being chronically over-paid, is born of a time when Heads saw no reason to dirty their hands with the business aspects of a school.

As a new and forward-thinking Head, it is essential for you to recognise that your school is indeed a business. With salaries accounting for perhaps 70% of outgoings and operating costs routinely running ahead of inflation, it is no surprise that bursars in independent schools occasionally look grumpy. You will do much to cement this relationship if you take the trouble to understand the broad financial principles on which the school operates and to work with your bursar to see that the best possible education is delivered within the framework of good business management.

There will be lively debate in the process, but this should happen well before your first governors' meeting. The board will then be delighted to see that you and the bursar – after all, the twin compasses by which their vision for the future of the school is being plotted – are working in such amicable partnership.

From this relationship follows that with the rest of the senior leadership team. Here, there are many different models and you may inherit something which works very well. Remember, though, that your own strengths will not necessarily be the same as your predecessor's, so in the eyes of your close senior colleagues, there may be the sense either that toes are being trodden on or that gaps are being left. Take your time to see the strengths of the people around you and to learn what they expect of you, before you embark on re-organisation and change. This may well be something to address towards the end of your first year.

Your arrival as the new Head may be greeted with some caution. If you are replacing a long-serving and much loved predecessor (and we all seem to!) it may, as we have seen, take time to win acceptance. But you are *new*. There is something inherently exciting about that: you bring fresh ideas, new possibilities, fresh air – and you *must* find opportunities during your first year to express that energy and enthusiasm as widely and as tangibly as possible.

This may be in person at your first staff meeting, in assemblies, at open events for parents as well as in writing in mailings or letters home. Beware, however, of being trapped into expounding your fully-formed vision for the future of the school at this stage. You probably don't have one yet (or if you do, you may not have done enough listening and will probably want to revise what you say later). What is important is to enthuse about the school as it is now: after all, you admired it enough to want to lead it and those people to whom you are speaking are all personally bound up in the school as it is. They want to know both that you affirm their school and that you have the drive and energy to take it forward in new and exciting ways.

Your thoughts on the future may well be incomplete at this stage and you can use the first year to seek opinion in a very open way that may be more difficult later. You might want to bring staff and governors together for a day of strategic thinking about the future direction of the school; planning such a day can achieve a real sense of focus and cohesion within the senior leadership team. You may want to survey parents, using a carefully tailored questionnaire. If you do this, be careful not to set up the expectation that every suggestion will be acted upon: you are merely gathering opinion about the strengths of the school to feed into longer term planning. Your more assertive parents will probably not need a questionnaire to prompt them to give you their opinions, but remember that the majority are the ones who normally tell you least and it is their views which should be of most interest.

Your relationship with the parent body as a new Head is one of the most difficult to establish and to gauge. Parents will be watching hawk-like to see what you will do – but above all, they want to know you and to have some sense of you as a person. All kinds of myths will have preceded you: when I arrived at SPGS, the word was that I was going to be incredibly strict and introduce the unthinkable concept of uniform. So it's helpful to deal with that quickly, by getting in front of parents (perhaps at an evening reception in year groups) and simply letting them hear you speak about yourself, your first impressions *etc*.

If there are normally regular letters home, this can be another good way to establish your own tone and personality in the parents' minds. Remember also that parents talk to one another a great deal. If you receive one of those two-page, closely typed catalogues of everything that needs sorting out in the school from a parent, news of your method of dealing with it will spread. Here is your opportunity to show that you are listening and that you take the views of parents seriously, without bending with every strong wind that happens to blow in your direction. School cultures vary, but it can also be a good thing to make time to see individual parents yourself, especially in that first year, if they have concerns. Later, you may need to delegate some of this to others, but a powerful message is conveyed if you are seen to give parents personal time.

I've managed to write half of this chapter without mentioning students, except in passing. This is no coincidence. As a new Head, the thing I noticed more than anything was how the demands of the job constantly took me away from the students and seemed almost to insulate me from their point of view. In retrospect, a key factor in this was that my office was in a somewhat far-flung spot and while the view of rolling acres of garden was delightful, it did not often feature the faces of the girls.

Now, at St Paul's, my office gives directly on to the main thoroughfare. The location is distinctly less peaceful but it keeps me much more in touch with students informally, day to day. If your office is in the wrong place – change it in Year One. If you don't, you will find too many reasons why it cannot happen.

There will be plenty of ways for you to make yourself known to your students and to connect with them. Take assemblies regularly: preparing them takes time, but the students will appreciate your visibility and you have an opportunity to convey something of your character, values and interests to them. If you especially enjoy teaching, go on doing some, but only if you can be certain you will be there. Nothing gives the sense that students are not your top priority faster than missing lessons. I personally very much enjoy my weekly meetings with the Head Girl Team of seven. We have no agenda, we eat a lot of chocolate and, listening to them talk, I gain an invaluable insight into what is *really* important in school that week.

Getting to know a whole school-full does take time and I find I rely on photographs as a reference point to fix someone firmly in my mind. Asking for a set of photographs of the staff in advance proved a great help in my recent move, where I was new to the school and knew absolutely no one. I was able to learn a good many names before arriving. People are reassured (and even occasionally touched) if you know their name, and you will know whose help to seek if all your bookshelves fall off the wall or your computer crashes.

Of course it will take longer to get to know all your new colleagues and here too, beware of the mythologies that you may have picked up in advance of your first term. That notoriously difficult head of department may just have been waiting for your particular approach to become much more compliant and another person's difficult colleague may not be yours. Greet the staff with an open mind, be determined to see the best in all of them (as you hope they will in you) and the very change you bring may be enough to smooth and settle some old schisms or entrenched attitudes. (Don't think this is your own magic, by the way – your successor will have the same effect on the issues you have failed to solve in a few years' time.)

It's easy, of course, to be pleasant to people in the first few months when, in a sense, you have yet to become responsible for the way things are. At the same time, the moment will come when you may have to insist on new ways of doing things which will not necessarily be popular. Facing people with change that may mean more is required of them, or that their comfort zone is threatened, is never easy – especially when everyone thought you were so nice. Another Head wisely and simply advised me that in dealing with difficulty, you only have to keep in mind the best interests of the students you are all there to serve. Keeping the students front of mind will always tell you your right course and give you the strength to pursue it.

With so much in front of you, what is there behind you to back you up? The governors; your PA and most importantly – your friends and family.

Styles of governance vary widely in independent schools, and I have been richly blessed in both my Headships with boards of governors whose approach has been to take an intelligent and informed interest in the school, to offer specialist professional advice when I have needed it but to remember that as charitable trustees, they have appointed me to lead the school and should, on the whole, let me get on with that independently.

In a new Headship you should take time to get to know your governors. Find out how you will report to them (usually in a written termly statement) and the sort of thing they want to know. Make your reports interesting and not too long. At board meetings, show them how much you are enjoying your role. Your energy and enthusiasm for the school will reassure them that they made the right choice (after a gruelling process which cost a fortune) and help them imagine you in your role with staff, parents and students.

If there is choppy water ahead: concern over pupil numbers, staffing difficulties, a long list of late payers, concern over the welfare of individuals – give them the unvarnished truth and do not hide anything. These are the people who will help you through difficult times (and there will be some) but they do not like surprises. Especially, they do not like to hear things about the school that they have not heard from you first. Show them you have courage – after all, they partly chose you for it – and they will back you. In the end, your governors may have a deep and lasting affection for the school but they are volunteers. They give of their time without salary and it is your job to ensure that their time is well used and productive.

Especially, they should always walk away from the school glad that they have placed it in your hands.

Within school, probably the most important relationship of all will be with your PA. If you are new to Headship, it may be that you have never had such a luxury before and are uncertain how to fulfil your part of this partnership. If you are lucky, and your PA knows the school well, you will find you have the perfect stage manager, who will wind you up and send you off to the right place at the right time, with the right bits of paper and generally regulate your life for you until you find your feet.

Working effectively with a PA is a chapter in itself, but I personally like to work to a set of basic principles. First, trust and confidentiality are essential. Your PA will see you at your worst (I guarantee it!) and will also see and prepare a great deal of sensitive and confidential information; it's vital therefore that you win this person's respect and loyalty and that you are certain he/she is proof against any staff room gossip.

A PA who is effective is also able to be pro-active: the idea is that your time is well managed and your in-box kept as low as possible. So encourage your PA to take initiative, think ahead and sort out problems if possible before they get to you. Part of managing your time is having a good gatekeeper, but at the same time the Head must guard against getting a reputation for never being available. You could try having 'open' or 'surgery' times when staff can drop in to see you without a formal appointment. A good PA will keep pressure away from you and, knowing you, will learn the kind of scheduling that you personally manage best: what kind of appointments you can cope with one after another, where you need a breather, *etc*.

As with governors, however, Heads do not like surprises, so encourage your PA not to 'protect' you from unpalatable information. This is the person with whom you will be able to share the finer and less fine moments, let off a little steam after a difficult meeting, trust to tell you when a letter you have dictated needs toning down and share a joke at the end of a difficult day. Treasure your PA, for her (or his) price is above rubies.

With all these relationships to feed and nurture, you may feel you have little left once you turn, as you will just occasionally, away from school and towards your friends and family. They will be very interested and understanding, but try not to talk about your new project all the time. You need a break from this endlessly fascinating set of moving pieces, and immersing yourself in the family, or in other people, or in your own outside interests, will restore you and give you new energy when you go back in to school. My own move to London this year has provided a marvellous outlet in the ready accessibility of galleries and theatres. All this I have drunk in thirstily, even if on leaving an exhibition I occasionally catch myself thinking 'I'll get a good assembly out of that!'

I began by saying that the key to the first year in any Headship was establishing strong relationships. Part of this, too, is learning more about oneself. Headship is demanding and potentially more stressful than virtually any other job, so it's important to recognise what you do best, what you find difficult or counter-intuitive, and what you are best not touching, but delegating to someone else.

Coming from a family of extroverts, it surprised me to recognise about myself, quite late, that I am actually a shy person who enjoys solitude. I now know that a formal dinner or social event with parents will take much more out of me than sitting down for two hours to write a speech. Understanding this, I can try to manage my time so that activities which are draining are balanced with those which, for me, are more reflective and can therefore refresh. Knowing yourself in this way will help you parcel out your energy and get to the end of that first year still glad you signed the contract.

If you are well into your first Headship and are considering a second, the great question is 'when?'. You are probably by nature a restless being (another thing I learned about myself) but do not be in too much of a rush. All kinds of factors may have a bearing on your decision but ideally, you should wait until your instinct about a particular new possibility is nothing less than irresistible. The course of one's experience in Headship is a curve: you have to invest huge energy during the start-up phase that we have been looking at when everything is unfamiliar; gradually you have the sense that you are beginning to 'happen' to the school and are making a difference and eventually comes the delicious feeling that you have arrived: it is your school at last, and the machinery is all spinning with a marvellous, effortless sweetness and the whole thing is in flight.

Management experts would say that this is when you should leave – but I disagree. You can fly along in this way for several years and really enjoy the sense of identity with the school that you have worked for. This is your best time and, helped by you, the school has become its best and true self. Of course, this does not last forever, so eventually your own spirit may draw you to some new challenge, some new difficulty. You will know when the move is the right one, but do not deny yourself the time to enjoy your first and perhaps most rewarding success – you have deserved it.

Much has been said and written in praise of Headship, yet there are still far too few people wanting to do it. Anyone reading this book must by definition be tempted, and I hope you will succumb. A strong and formative influence for all of us who have taken the step will have been the example of the mentors and role models who have helped us and inspired us earlier in our careers. For me there have been several, but once again, I acknowledge with respect and affection both Audrey Butler, Headmistress of Queenswood 1983-1996, who taught me so much and Elizabeth Diggory, High Mistress of St Paul's Girls' School 1998-2006.

Elizabeth sadly died of cancer in 2007 only months after her retirement and I dedicate my contribution to her memory.

Chapter 3

Staff

Bernard Trafford

What kind of leader do you want to be? It's a question that needs consideration, because the leadership style you adopt will be probed and tested – and never more thoroughly than by your teaching staff. Will you be a visionary? Slave-driver? Sergeant-major? Shoulder to cry on? Actually, you will probably be required to be all of these at different times.

There will always be occasions when morale is flagging and when you need to rally your troops in the manner of Henry V: at other times you will be more like a sheepdog, snapping at their heels. As sergeant-major, you'll be tut-tutting because no one else is apparently checking on the pupils' uniform or punctuality. And sometimes you'll be called upon to act as mentor, career coach, marriage-guidance expert or bereavement counsellor.

But all those labels – even that of visionary – are somewhat shallow. What will really define your Headship is the way in which you approach the job, day in, day out; how you walk your talk; the extent to which the values that drive your vision for your school and your chosen method of achieving it match your conduct around school; the way you interact with pupils and parents; and, above all, your dealings with your teachers.

Teachers are a fascinating, charming, entertaining, contradictory, frustrating, infuriating group of people. They are talented and highly committed. They see their job as a vocation, and they are generally insulted by any suggestion that they might merely be doing a job for which they are paid. Of course, the best of them do indeed give of their talents, energy and sheer inspiration in a measure far beyond anything that can be quantified in terms of salary.

So the Head is always treading a fine line between chivvying the dilatory and lauding the selfless and excellent. That's why one of the first rules of Headship must be never to indulge in collective blame. The notice in the staff room complaining about teachers' failure to complete some task or meet a deadline is a scattergun approach that hurts and offends the dedicated, and usually goes way over the head of the culprits!

But that doesn't mean that you cannot confront what is wrong. On the contrary, you must never walk past something with which you feel uncomfortable. Don't persuade yourself that you'll do something about it later: you probably won't. The Head sets the tone, so you must act (and be *seen* to act) when it's off-key. This is truly walking the talk. You set policy and strategy from the lofty position of the big desk in your study, but it is by walking about that you feel the quality and gauge the depth.

There are consolations: not only does getting out and about from the office bring you into contact (of a pleasant and informal kind) with your pupils, but teachers are invariably pleased to see you noting what they are doing well: "catching people doing things right", as management guru Tom Peters says, to the delight and uplift of those you encounter.

Management by walking about (MaBWA) was a mantra some years ago. I've tried to take it a stage further. Inspired by Peters, I call my approach PALP – *Poncing about looking pleased.* Seeing you on the move, your teachers will also be aware that you'll probably notice if they're a bit late for registration or for the start of a lesson. You're not the school Rotweiler: if that job needs doing, send for your deputy! No: you're not policing, merely sampling.

Then they'll know that, if something jars, grates against the ethos of which you are both architect and guardian, you'll respond. A brief word solves a problem while it's still small: telling the truth, certainly, but quietly – and without using it as an excuse to hurt. In short, *they'll* know that *you* know what's going on: that gives you real (rather than positional) authority when you try to implement change.

That's important, because you will certainly have to lead change – something to which teachers can be highly resistant. Schools are driven to change, constantly if unwillingly, by outside pressures. New patterns or styles of examinations; new subjects; bright new government ideas about producing more healthy, virtuous or productive citizens; political hostility; demand for evidence of public benefit; local or national economic downturn; competition from other schools; demographic decline. All of these, and more, can force capricious change on a school. You'll have your own agenda for change, too. Your brief as Head is to improve the school, to keep it developing, growing, moving forward.

All that means changing how things are done at present. And teachers, highly articulate and eminently plausible, are capable of finding countless reasons not to change. So what sort of leader, if any, can *lead change*? I like two of Howard Gardner's models of leadership *(Leading minds: an anatomy of leadership,* 1996): the *lead professional* and the *story-teller*. Teachers are comfortable with the lead professional: indeed, the only thing they can conceive of as being worse than having a Head in the first place, is the thought of having one who has no background in teaching!

As a former teacher you have some moral authority. In the past you must, they assume, have suffered as they do those torrid Friday afternoons when no one wanted to work; dealt with that intractable, stroppy 15 year-old; had the nightmares about teaching the wrong topic (and woken up to find you have!). And if you've risen to the top (the reasoning goes), you must once have been quite good at teaching.

That rather predictable teacher attitude is useful to you: it gives you credibility. Of course you are now very largely damned, having crossed the divide into Management, but you speak the language and you can show you still understand the pressures. So you can appeal to your colleagues' professionalism, to their care for the children they teach, to their ambition to see the school shine through the achievements of its pupils, as well as sympathising from your own experience with the things that make them groan. Presumably any change is for the greater good of the school and the people in it? (If it isn't, don't even start, because it's not worth the pain.) So you share the vision of where the school needs to go, 'better for all of us'.

That's what *ownership*, the buzz-word of change management, means. The more you manage to get the staff as a whole to share the vision and to share in planning its development, the greater the ownership, the richer the sense of shared endeavour, the smaller and less bitter the opposition. That's where you become the *story-teller*. You describe the vision; remind everyone of its virtues (and of the way everyone agreed they share it); and, when the going gets tough, remind them again.

One of the most powerful aspects of Churchill's wartime speeches was the fact that he did not pretend things were easy: but while he reminded his listeners that "blood, toil, tears and sweat" lay ahead, he never failed to refresh and share his vision of the ultimate victory, of the sunny uplands beyond the horizon. Churchill was the great story-teller, as well as the heroic leader.

Perhaps this sounds manipulative, but I don't believe it is. Indeed, it is about more than merely *sharing* the vision: it is about involving the whole staff, as far as you are able, in developing, defining and sharpening the vision in the first place. Focus groups and surveys may serve to identify the hopes and anxieties your staff share: self-destructing working groups (which do a specified job and then dissolve) are a useful means of pulling all the strands together, working out a coherent picture and planning a way forward. Then, with your senior colleagues and/or governors, you can develop the detailed strategy.

If you manage to work in this way, your teaching colleagues don't just get on board the ship: they have helped build the craft itself. Once launched, it is certainly your job to keep your hand on the tiller and to hold the course, even when tempest strikes or uncertainty causes determination to falter. At those times, you have to cling to the moral high ground: I've lost count of the times that I have said to my staff: "Look, we all agreed this is the way we need to go. We have to keep our nerve and keep working at it consistently". As the lead professional, who can demonstrate that you have consulted and listened, you speak with authority both professional and positional, steady the nerves and keep everyone on track.

Any vision for the school's future must, almost by definition, involve making it a better place. So at the heart of your vision and strategy lies school improvement. Part of that, of course, is improving the teaching.

Don't be afraid to get involved in detailed discussion about what happens in classrooms; how children are treated and how they feel about lessons; how teachers cater for their different learning styles or specific learning difficulties, even in the most high-powered academic school; how teachers' approaches vary with regard to assessment, to marking, to motivation, to dealing with de-motivated students.

All this is the very stuff of education, which is at the heart of your vision for the school. You are in charge and you must be involved. If you have succeeded in gaining a good level of buy-in from staff to the overall vision and to the strategic plan for achieving it, you have more than a right to discuss *in detail* the teaching and learning that are going on: you have a duty to do so, and teachers will acknowledge that fact, even if they don't always welcome it.

The alternative, after all, is that you become involved only in tedious and ultimately sterile discussions about which examination board to adopt; whether IGCSE is better than GCSE in certain subjects; whether Pre-U is going to catch on; and how many reports or parents' evenings you should have in a year. These are merely decisions about assessment and qualifications, and don't go to the heart of the education or the school life for which you are responsible.

So you need to take a close interest in the development of your staff, in their personal/professional growth as well as their deployment. To be sure, you hold them accountable for performance: but they will hold you accountable in turn for nurturing their career. This starts the moment you appoint them – "the most important thing a Head does", I was once told. It's certainly pretty crucial, and I was surprised when, a few years ago, an experienced deputy at another school told me that his Head left all the appointments to him. When I raised an eyebrow he suggested I had a problem in delegating (that's a charge levelled at all Heads when they become harassed and over-busy).

I don't think that making appointments is something that can be delegated. I make sure that I am involved in the production of advertisements and job descriptions, not to mention the supporting paperwork, of which we provide a huge amount. All this is designed so that the job we offer is attractive, and so that the candidates arrive for interview fired up and eager to win the job. They work hard to get it: nowadays I make them teach a sample lesson, and they are interviewed by a group of students as well as by my colleagues and me. I make them wait in school while we make our decision, and the panel deliberates until there is unanimity or at least very strong consensus around the table about the candidate we want.

As a result, those involved in making appointments, particularly heads of department, know there has been a thorough process and that they have got the candidate they want. The successful candidate has battled for the job and feels a strong personal loyalty both to me as Head and to the other staff who helped select them. It's a powerful and positive process: much better, I think, than leaving the candidate to make the long journey home (during which I, for one, have always spent the time convincing myself why I wouldn't have wanted the job anyway, in case I didn't get offered it) and then wait for a phone call some hours or even days later. It's all about motivation, in effect.

Having gathered teachers around you with that strong personal loyalty to you as Head, you need to look after them! Of course you will have a director of studies who will be checking on the quality of teaching, and on the results pupils achieve; and you will also have someone in charge of continuing professional development (CPD). But you'll want to know that the teachers themselves feel that someone is keeping an eye on their personal and career development.

One way of doing this is through an appraisal system. I meet fellow Heads who reckon to have a face-to-face discussion with every colleague in the course of, say, a two-year appraisal cycle. I can never decide whether to be awestruck or dubious: I just know I wouldn't manage that. But I do speak annually to every head of department, who brings completed appraisal forms from every member of the department so that achievements, hopes, fears and frustrations are all brought to my attention – and, if any personal follow-up is needed, naturally I make arrangements to talk to the particular teacher. It's not the only way of doing it, but it works for me. And those conversations are frequently fruitful in identifying those colleagues who need opportunities to take on additional responsibility and exercise leadership – and in spotting ways to provide them.

That kind of appraisal conversation is a formalisation, perhaps, of an open-door policy. Most Heads claim to have a door that is always open to staff. I have known Common Rooms where it was said of their Head's boasted accessibility: 'open door, closed mind.' There is a moral there: if you are serious about inviting staff to contribute ideas, as well as to off-load worries, you need to be prepared to listen and to take action on what you hear. Sometimes your efforts to get work done will be frustrated by the number of colleagues who want to get things off their chest before the end of a long term. It's maddening! But it may be good for the school, even if it means that you end up absorbing other people's stress.

I have a personal rule that helps me through those times when a colleague appears in my doorway, usually late in the week and term, and unloads a deluge of anger or disappointment about how they are undervalued and unfairly treated, how the school and (explicitly or by implication) my management are failing dismally and blighting people's lives. As the one-sided tirade progresses (and I resolutely remind myself that my open door policy encourages this sort of disclosure and that *it is a good thing*, even on a Friday) a feeling of depression settles on me.

"Am I really getting it all *so* wrong?" I wonder. Then a small voice whispers in my head, "One of us is barmy, and I don't think it's me". At that moment the other person will invariably say something so biased or off-the-wall that I am immediately reassured: it *is* an entirely one-sided view that is being presented. This sounds smug, perhaps, but it happens time and again, and at such moments I say to myself: "The rule has proved itself again". At the end they usually say, "Well, I feel better now!" as the burden is shifted, for the moment, from their shoulders to mine. But the burden is bearable: the voice has whispered its message to me and the balance is restored.

All this may make it look as if you are on your own as Head. Of course you're not: I'm not writing the recipe for a one-man [*sic*] miracle Headship! Every Head nowadays is supported by a senior management team. There is no one right shape for this team, and you may find over the years that changed circumstances call for a different structure. If so, be confident enough to change it, if your governors will let you. Perhaps one danger to avoid is the temptation to surround yourself with ever more managers as you spot more jobs that need doing: management creep happens all too easily!

The picture I have painted of a Head very much in contact with the teaching staff does not reflect an obsessively hands-on approach, or an unwillingness to delegate. On the contrary, a well-ordered management structure, where everyone knows what their job entails and does it, should leave you free to make and maintain the personal relationships with your staff that are so necessary. You depend on your senior team to free you from swathes of routine tasks so that you can deal with the people on a human, not an administrative, level.

The better the team, the more tempting it may be to seek company within it. When a close-knit senior team is really working well, it's very exciting, and comforting too: you begin to think you can achieve anything. Be aware, though, that you will have several ambitious people within the team. You will have spotted those with untapped leadership potential, and will want to give them a chance to develop further – but promotions and rivalries can create tensions and put a strain on the working relationship. So remember to give them time to go back to the Common Room. You have crossed the great divide, but they still have at least one foot back there among their teacher colleagues and they don't want to lose their roots; not yet, at any rate. So let them go, and accept the loneliness of Headship at times.

Amid your senior team will be your bursar. Another chapter will deal with that particular relationship, but it is worth stressing how important the Head's role is in bringing together the teaching and non-teaching sides of the school. Although the bursar invariably heads what we nowadays call the support staff (a more attractive term than non-teaching), you can do a great deal to make sure that all those other hard workers in your school don't feel second-best – and you can try to prevent busy or impatient teachers from treating them inconsiderately. That happens all too easily.

In your work with teachers you will experience some of your greatest frustrations – but some of the most profound satisfaction too. Notwithstanding the fact that your mission is to educate children, working with your intellectual peers, with the top-class professionals we tend to attract in our schools, is full of stimulation, excitement, challenge, good humour and endless variety. Whether it's an uproarious gathering in the pub following a major school inspection, or an intense meeting planning intellectual developments, with keen minds buzzing and interacting, the experience of leading a close-knit, loyal band of teachers brings some of most acute pleasures of Headship.

Chapter 4

Curriculum Strategy

Sarah Evans

As Head, you have to believe that what goes on in your school is of fundamental importance to the positive development of the children and young people. If a child achieves five top grades at A Level, the experience needs to have been as rich and enjoyable as if he or she leaves with Es or no grades at all. There is more to education than being constantly in the thrall of national dictates, the exam boards, and parental pressures. Not only must you believe that, but you must keep saying so to everyone all the time – to colleagues, to parents and students.

Prospectuses, websites and talks on Open Days all dwell on the extra-curricular range and achievements, the moral and social values and in one form or another, exam results. The hard core of school, the curriculum, is surprisingly low profile – and yet above all else this is why a school is a school and not a sports club, performing arts centre or church. Indeed 'subjects' have for so long been regarded as old fashioned, that it must be time they had a comeback – so I shall start by looking at the Head's leadership of the mainstream curriculum, before moving to the more fashionable areas of assessment, extra-curricular activities and the hidden curriculum.

First: how much should an independent school seek to follow what maintained sector schools do, in curriculum terms? This is part of a wider question about the degree of independence which any school should have to make its own decisions. As a country, we cannot make up our minds about the academic provision offered by schools. Should we have a largely proscribed standard school curriculum, or should there be considerable variation, leaving many decisions up to individual schools?

The same holds within a subject: how far should there be national schemes of work, or how far should the detail be left to individual teachers? The reason why we have vacillated is of course because, frustratingly for politicians and some educationalists, there is not actually a right answer.

When the National Curriculum of 1988 was adopted, with its guiding principle of a broad and balanced curriculum for all, many independent schools felt this is what they had long been providing. Independent schools could differentiate themselves as offering the National Curriculum Plus. They had a huge advantage: freedom from statutory obligations if they wanted it, for individuals or because of the nature of their school.

Now that the National Curriculum has been replaced, at least post-14, with a more flexible approach, and there is new emphasis on personalised learning, the challenge facing the independent sector is to show it is still offering something better. Educational leadership is not just about your own individual school, it is about differentiating the sector in a very positive way from the state system: lighting beacons that our freedom gives us that can then be picked up and shared.

Where the curriculum is concerned, what you never have is a blank piece of paper. Before you were ever thought about, the piece of paper has been written on by the heavy pen of school tradition, national examination strategy and parental expectations. But you can still dream, and the guiding vision behind your leadership may be helped if you consider your ideal curriculum for the particular school before becoming too immersed in micro-management.

Second: there is the question of how narrowly 'useful' education should be. After the huge publicity which heralded the introduction of the first National Curriculum, there was much discussion about what to include – but even then, a lot more around the detail than big ideas themselves. In recent years the emphasis has been on pedagogy: on how children learn and how we assess it, on how to use technology effectively and where technology might take us in the future.

The justification for the actual subject matter is not much examined, and one consequence has been perhaps to make children's education vulnerable to a take-over by those whose main pre-occupation is utilitarian education in its narrow sense. Because few people are prepared to stand up and say why history or physics are important *in themselves*, it has been easy for the pragmatists to argue that giving difficult 14 year-olds a course in tourism is quite obviously preferable to understanding physical geography.

It has also been argued that a skills-based approach to education is the best preparation for life. Skills, it is argued, are transferable in a way that the traditional subject knowledge approach isn't. The subjects which children follow are therefore of less importance than the generic skills being taught. A Head will usually find both points of view among colleagues, and often within a single department – a potential source of some conflict. So a Head needs to indicate where their personal sympathies lie.

Any curricular choices that you make need to be very carefully explained to parents so they know what they are buying into. Parents have a tendency to see themselves as consumers of education, much as they are consumers of food. They should be able to have what they fancy and leave the rest. Unless you want your curriculum to change with every new cohort, you have to make it clear what the expectations are. Schools do have a responsibility beyond what a particular parent thinks is right for her child.

The very fact that independent schools, unlike their maintained sector counterparts, have considerable freedom arguably makes the sector more vulnerable to these ever-changing market forces. It is worth ensuring that parents are absolutely clear what the curriculum parameters are, so as to avoid endless disagreements once a child is with you. There may be curriculum areas that most parents believe their child should be able to opt out of, but which you consider you have a duty to a wider society to maintain. Classics would be an example – or German or Russian.

Third: there is the whole question of personalised education, in the wake of the Tomlinson Report's call for 'flexible pathways' and the

Gilbert Review into 2020 Education. A new Head will probably want to examine the degree to which a curriculum is in practise flexible enough to meet individual needs. Personalised learning, now a buzz phrase in the state sector, is something that has been one of the traditional strengths of independent schools. An examination of how flexible your curriculum can be usually shows there are many limitations, particularly around finance. If you conclude that a broad and balanced curriculum for all is to the detriment of responding to individual needs, you are faced with the financial reality of providing more groups, smaller classes and everything that goes with them.

Fourth: there will always be questions about assessments – especially in a world in which the exam boards have increasingly been driven by market forces. While the iron fist of state control appears to be lifting from the curriculum, it continues to exert its force in the area of assessment. It can be argued that the problems of the curriculum have not been to do with any particular subject and its suitability, or with issues of mass consumption, but with the single model of assessment – GCSE and A level. While lip service is paid to assessment for learning – using our assessment to help each child forward in the best possible way – we are all heavily involved in that process of sifting for a meritocracy – standardized national examinations.

It is this that perhaps offers at the moment the greatest degree of freedom for the independent sector. Everyone is now aware that many people in secondary education do not regard GCSEs and A levels as satisfactory. Nor do those who may be described as the end users. So independent schools have increasingly looked at different qualifications, and there is currently (2007) much debate around IB, the Cambridge Pre-U, IGCSEs, fewer GCSEs, less course work and so on. As things stand, state schools have very limited choice – although it will be interesting to see how soon the DCSF sees variety of provision as a competitive advantage that can be extended to the state sector.

The arguments, in which a new Head will be well versed, for and against the various exams, are partly pragmatic and partly curricular. If your competitive edge has fallen because your students are not doing so well nationally in external exams, you may be well advised to look at alternatives. Much has been made of the feminisation of exams to account for the mysterious change in the traditional position of boys doing best in most things except perhaps food science. So you may decide to look for an exam in which your boys would do better. The arcane arts of picking the easiest exam board is one in which many heads of department are well versed. Others take a higher-minded approach and argue that the shallowness of the exam curriculum is leading to a dumbing-down of teaching itself. Since these external assessments are a way of controlling the curriculum, the link is well made.

Then there are wider curriculum questions. A lively area of debate for many staff rooms is the amount of cross-curricular activity that should be introduced. Enterprise learning and citizenship are the sort of thematic approaches that are popular along with the more established personal, social and moral education. The amount of time that can be devoted to these, the degree to which they are covered in existing areas, the need for lengthy audits to establish who is doing what, may be necessary where the latest trend has been added as a bolt-on to the already over-crowded curriculum.

A feature of British education has always been a belief that it is more than just a number of academic subjects delivered in a classroom. The idea of a liberal education, where a school is concerned with the development of the whole child, runs through much of this country's educational thinking. The extra-curricular programme is seen as a co-existing extension of lessons to enrich children's lives. For a long time, these programmes have been regarded as something of the prerogative of the independent sector, and another of its competitive edges over its maintained counterpart. The state sector is now introducing its extended schools agenda: it will be interesting to see how this develops.

The range and quality of extra-curricular activities are key factors in discriminating between schools. Traditionally it has been teachers who have run these, with input from senior pupils. Some activities spring naturally from traditional academic subjects – for example, a creative writing group. These tend to continue from generation to generation:

drama and music flourish outside the classroom because schools will have music and English teachers. Others come about because of the particular interests of teachers that have nothing to do with a subject – so a chess club may be run by an art teacher because that is how she spends her leisure time.

A Head may need to decide how far to control this. Can it all be left to individual passions and enthusiasms, or is there a hard-core of activities that a school must offer – even if no-one is particularly keen on doing it. What do you do if your music department are all jazz enthusiasts and no one cares about English church music? How important is this? Some people are genuinely attracted to teaching because they see it as allowing them to combine an all-absorbing interest with something that will earn a living. Sport might be a good example, and Heads may be able to dangle extra-curricular possibilities in front of desirable candidates.

There is a current view that teachers should be paid to do what they are trained to do. Running the Graphic Universe Club is not what they are trained for: the argument goes you can't expect a teacher to do the sort of preparation and marking now required if they are also producing three school plays. If they have time on their hands, they should be running catch-up lunchtime sessions or extension after-school lectures to convert those Grade B candidates into the all important Grade A students.

Even within the independent sector, where this thinking has been far less prevalent than in the state sector, you will find plenty of teachers who will argue they are under too much academic pressure to commit to other activities and that, in any case, as children move towards external exams, they should largely focus on getting their course work in and revising.

You may find you need to pay teachers to take on extra-curricular activities – though many independent schools have contracts that indicate that extra-curricular work is part of the job. Some schools have approached the difficulty of getting staff to commit to extra-curricular activities by employing non-teachers to run some of them. The state sector seems to be doing this too in its out-of-hours learning programme. Some areas are more consistently easy to staff like this than others.

Sports coaches and peripatetic musicians can usually be employed, but the philosophy group or the fungi forage weekends can be harder.

Without doubt, there is a huge pressure on schools to deliver in this area. Parents will often see independent education as an alternative to spending their every waking out-of-school-time driving children here, there and everywhere to ensure they do all the things middle class children are supposed to do. If a school can provide on site enough of these, it has a distinct edge. But at some stage you have to decide how much, why and for whom. If you have staff who are there because they love this aspect, that is fine, but you can't guarantee that the next appointments you make will have the same enthusiasms.

But if discovering someone to conduct the choir is a problem, it is nothing compared with one other major issue: trying to manage the hidden curriculum. This can be defined as 'what children learn when no one is noticing'. Schools have a hidden curriculum whether they like it or not, and a Head has to decide how much management it needs. A new Head, arriving at a school that is facing difficulties, can find that actively managing the hidden curriculum will turn things around. But it can also be a hugely controversial area where there is less consensus among colleagues than you might reasonably have expected.

You can usually discover something of the hidden curriculum by information that is out in the public domain. A website or prospectus may imply whether academic achievement is all important. It may indicate whether there is a zero tolerance approach to transgressions, or whether a more liberal attitude prevails. You can probably quickly pick up how far the school is driven by a belief in competition – houses, competitions, prizes, merit orders of all sorts will tell you. These may well be areas you have considered carefully before you took up a post. Many visitors to schools, particularly those who frequently see different schools, will say that they can sense what a school is like from the moment they walk through the front door. As an applicant for Headship, you will have been very sensitive to this, but it is easy to forget it once you have been in post a few months.

This area of human values, of friendliness, openness, welcome, respect, interest in others, courtesy, the atmosphere of a school, is what comes across on a daily basis to children. For some it can offer an alternative model to home life. But while everyone on your staff will probably subscribe to the sort of values mentioned above, if asked, you may find that their behaviour is far from compatible with them. It is here that you can often find that human nature does not fit neatly into hidden curriculum management.

Let us say that you, as a staff, have agreed that you must speak with one voice, sing from the same hymn sheet or whatever metaphor you choose, to describe a unanimous agreement about fundamental values. A member of staff comes to you outraged by a child's rudeness and demands that you demonstrate your support by instantly suspending the child. Clearly the child has been rude – and you are all agreed courtesy is fundamental to showing our respect for everyone. But on questioning the child and those who watched the drama unfold, it becomes obvious the child was taunted by the member of staff and pushed into a psychological corner with no room to manoeuvre other than to be rude. What is the hidden curriculum if you support the child – or the member of staff?

The deeper you explore this aspect of school life, the more complex (and therefore more absolutely fascinating) it becomes. Even more than the question of whether you make everyone do design and technology, the area will rouse high emotions. A new Head may well consider how far to set out the stall in this area immediately, opening up possible and perhaps unnecessary controversy or let it be revealed bit by bit through the actions taken and hope that those actions will speak for themselves in a practical way.

So, as a Head, you have to be tactically astute to balance a whole set of demands and variables. The changes of direction in the state sector indicate that, as a society, we have yet to make up our minds about how far a curriculum should respond to the market, or how far it should be led by other guiding principles. Your preparation for Headship may have clarified your position, and although you cannot change curricula overnight, it is worth making clear anything on which you are unlikely to shift.

Apart from macro-management of the curriculum, there is a lot of micro-management that seems to be drawn to the Head like a magnet. Most Heads don't get involved in the nitty-gritty of who teaches Year 10 last thing on a Thursday afternoon, and save their skills for agreeing how many physics lessons a week are justified. But it never does to forget the power of the timetabler. I once arrived at a school where four heads of department, including the timetabler, had non-contact time all Friday afternoon – and had done so for as long as anyone could remember. They were a golfing four and that was their regular weekly game.

There are a number of timetable models around and guidance available on how to fit the quart that is the curriculum into the pint pot that is the timetable. Although you will not want to get bogged down in the details, it is important to understand the basis on which a particular school constructs its timetable, and it is worth considering sitting in on the process in your first year. It will give you an overview of the implications of change in one area on other areas.

It is valuable to talk over any possible changes with the person responsible for timetabling early on, because it is frustrating to plan initiatives, only to be told the timetable won't allow it. Having said that, the timetable is the tool of the curriculum and not the other way round, whatever the problems of managing the change may be.

Where is it all leading, as pupils move up the school? Universities vacillate. Some will claim they want well-rounded students, who have done more than just got a good set of A levels. Others may pay lip service to this, but in fact want the best mathematicians, historians or classicists they can get – and you don't get to be one of them by spending all weekend on the rugby pitch.

After a few terms in, will you, Wordsworth-like, be asking 'Whither is it fled, the visionary gleam / Where is it now the glory and the dream'? Heads need to consider how to keep the dream alive, and it is different for each of us. Some will find it in their own reading, others by attending conferences and courses, talking to inspiring colleagues or joining on-line professional support groups. There is no lack of external support –

in fact the problem is more likely to be discriminating between the good and bad of what is on offer.

In one sense new ideas crowd round the education world like fruit flies round a bowl of strawberries. Everyone feels at times that it is difficult to keep up with every new report and initiative. But, as with other aspects of your leadership, it is not about you knowing everything and driving everything. You have colleagues around you with their own expertise, knowledge, particular interests and missions. The fun of Headship is garnering all that, for the good of the children.

Chapter 5

Curriculum Management

Things a new Head needs to know
but probably won't have the time to ask…

Brenda Despontin

Barely will a new Head have had enough time to unpack the boxes, or to arrange the family photographs on her desk, before the visits start. Heads of department will call by, ostensibly to welcome their new leader, but will invariably take the opportunity to 'flag up a few issues'. It soon becomes apparent that managing both the curriculum itself, and those colleagues who manage the subjects within it, is a complex but essential competency for every Head.

Decisions about who meets what learning opportunity, in which venue to be taught by whom, lie at the heart of why schools exist. Get the decisions right and the pupils will be challenged, stimulated and excited by their teaching and learning. Get them wrong and the curriculum becomes expensive, limiting or inappropriate – not fit for purpose.

What should they learn? One size will never fit all where curriculum provision is concerned. Much depends on the ability range of the pupils, customer expectations of the parents and governors, size of the cohorts, and availability of funding, facilities and expertise. Our independence liberates us from the restrictions of a National Curriculum with its attendant testing, and ensures we retain endangered curriculum areas such as classics, modern foreign languages and physics.

However, we ignore developments in the maintained sector at our peril: our boys and girls leave us to compete in a global market, with their peers educated to contribute to a skills-based economy and a techno-savvy workplace. Emerging markets in Asia, the Far East, or South America are planning strategically to ensure their schools will produce a workforce equipped for tomorrow's world. In countries such as Dubai and Qatar, investment in education is equalled only by that in the construction industry.

We must be sure, then, that our cynicism, and our desire sometimes to adhere to a traditional pedagogy, do not penalise our pupils' search for a place in a world where the employment experience, and indeed the opportunities, will be very different from our own.

Heads arrive in a school with diverse experiences of curriculum management on which to draw. A previous role as director of studies or curriculum deputy may mean a good knowledge of options and timetabling, but the hard decisions will have invariably been the Head's. Others new in post may have risen through the pastoral ranks, and be nervous about the implications of funding and staffing subjects.

New Heads are well advised not to promise too much too soon: it is a juggling of pupils' needs with resources, a matching of mission statement and vision with the more pragmatic, bottom line budgeting, and is often far more complicated than the hard-nosed business folk of the governing body imagine. For example, a cursory glance at class size at A2 in a 'minority' subject such as music technology, design technology, Latin or textiles may indicate an immediate and obvious cost centre where savings can be made.

However, the very fact that those subjects are available fulfils the school's publicised strategic priority to provide breadth and balance. Pupils sign on for the sixth form to study maths or languages precisely because those other subjects are on offer too. If they were not, the sixth form college just up the road will most certainly offer them, and the customers are lost to the competition. When reviewing the curriculum, it is vital to balance the books for any school's survival. The vast majority of our schools do not have the luxury of huge surpluses or endowments to prop up the expensive cost centres, of which the staff salary bill is by far the most significant.

Speaking to *The Times* about his period in office as Prime Minister, Tony Blair said: "The hardest thing about Leadership is learning to ignore the loudest voices". The same is true for new Heads. Before succumbing to the plausible plans of the more vocal staff, arguing so eloquently for a fifth set in Year 8, for more non-contact time, or for another ICT suite, a new Head would be well advised to undertake a full curriculum review.

The curriculum committee tasked to do this, chaired by the deputy responsible for this area of school life, might include a few pillars of staff-room wisdom, but it will benefit equally from some younger staff, perhaps given specific areas to research, such as the potential impact on the school of the International Baccalaureate, the desirability of IGCSEs, or reporting on Diplomas. Feedback to heads of departments' meetings and full staff meetings is a good professional development opportunity in itself, but it also ensures all staff remain *au fait* with up-to-date developments in other schools and FE colleges, sometimes providing a salutary glimpse outside the comfort zone. It encourages an awareness of the bigger picture, including an idea about operating costs.

For the same reason, the regular, excellent briefing papers from the joint Education and Academic Policy committee of HMC/GSA, and from the Universities sub-committee, are worth circulating to all departments in a school. Their essential guide to trends and future developments at QCA and the DCSF, together with the accurate information on admissions procedures, make them an essential part of a Head's toolkit for steering the curriculum. Like Janus, a Head has to keep in view those historical aspects of the school's teaching and learning which customers sought in the first place when they signed up perhaps ten years ago, and which gave the school its fine reputation as a place of academic excellence, but one must turn the other way too – to face the future, and be not just up-to-date, but preparing for the pupils not yet on the roll.

The curriculum review, if it is worth its salt, will raise predictable questions, all of which lie at the heart of curriculum management. If a school has its own junior department, for example, will there be PIPS testing, or KS2, or tailor-made, in-house versions? To what extent will the heads of department in the senior section liaise with junior colleagues on curriculum content to avoid overlap? Will/should the timetable facilitate some senior staff teaching younger pupils? How will academic tracking in the junior school influence setting in Year 7?

On the other hand, schools which depend chiefly on intake at 13+ have special decisions to make involving close liaison with prep school directors of studies over Common Entrance requirements. For schools which attract entrants from a range of backgrounds there may be staffing and cost implications, as the pupils arrive in Year 9 with or without a second language to that level. Again, the decisions are often not immediately obvious. Appointing a teacher to provide a few new 13+ entrants with 'catch up' German lessons might appear expensive – until the income from their full boarding fees is taken into consideration, and it could mean the difference between whether they accept a place or not.

Curriculum planning decisions start seriously in Year 7 and are revisited each year afterwards. Should the pupils all encounter as many subject areas as possible to whet the academic appetite, and so provide as wide a range of learning experiences as can be incorporated (and funded) before option choices become a reality? Or do young learners benefit from deeper learning and substantial exploration, but in fewer subjects, perhaps timetabled imaginatively to facilitate greater flexibility? Should our schools be more creative in curriculum provision for Years 7-9 than in the past – allowing for more cross-curricular projects perhaps – or for whole periods of a school day where technology might link pupils to other learners elsewhere in the global classroom, or for more individualised, 'personalised' learning time? What can a Head do to keep the notoriously difficult Year 9 motivated and stimulated, challenged and channelled, especially after the Year 10 choices are made?

Many independent schools educate boys and girls with a wide ability range, some of whom may have English as a second language. The decision then required is whether or not to celebrate and market this aspect of the school's culture, offering vocational or skills-based courses, and employing specialists for small sets of intensive support teaching. The attraction for a Head lies in increasing the numbers on roll, and therefore income, by widening the ability range at intake, or by removing any academic entrance assessment altogether, an extremely alluring option at a time of falling rolls, better state provision and an ever-more demanding customer base.

But experienced colleagues would caution: handle with care. Such measures change a school's ethos, and hidden curriculum costs might undermine any immediate advantages. They need careful management. Consider first: how many extra pupils will be required to balance those expensive staff/student ratios? Will there be sufficient classroom space, boarding beds, or specialist resources? How many extra computers are needed? Will the eventual downturn in examination results matter to the traditional customer base, which may drift away as a result? These are important decisions and can ultimately determine the survival of a school, or its demise.

Years 10 and 11 bring examinations, and further important decisions. The question as to which subjects belong in a core group at that point in a pupil's academic journey would again benefit from debate in the new Head's Curriculum review. With the advent of Diplomas, Heads might wish to explore sharing curriculum opportunities through partnership opportunities with neighbouring maintained schools, or to seek links electronically with other independent schools offering expensive minority subjects online.

State schools have delivered parts of their curriculum via video-link for some years. It broadens the subject choice available, and pupils are engaged in imaginative, collaborative learning opportunities. Replacing teachers with machines to impart knowledge smacks of a brave new school world which many Heads abhor and will fight to resist, but when it comes to exploring alternatives outside the traditional box, independent school Heads undoubtedly lag behind their colleagues in the maintained sector. The curriculum of the future is probably limited only by the technology accessible in a school, the enthusiasm and expertise of the staff, and the vision of the head to mastermind its deployment.

For the immediate present, decisions for Years 10 and 11 centre around issues such as offering triple or dual award science, or both, with all the attendant questions about lab availability and number of technicians. In a world where the expectation for outstanding keyboard skills is a given in every career and every university course, and where maintained schools highlight their importance, in a world where the first of the specialised Diplomas is offered in ICT, should an independent school Head insist on GCSE ICT (or equivalent) for all?

Is there a case for staffing fast-track AS (in Music for example), or offering GCSE dance or PE, or for moving to IGCSEs, in maths or science perhaps, but at the expense of the school's league-table position? How many GCSEs are desirable/affordable in the school? What best meets the pupils' needs in ways which can be funded and resourced appropriately? At every turn, the Head's final judgement will influence the budget, but these decisions also impact on the learning experience of the students, and ultimately the culture and reputation of the school. They extend even to the morale and job security of the staff.

At Key Stage 4 there are also the debates about the timing of mock examinations: hold them before Christmas and the music/drama staff are apoplectic; hold them in January and many smaller schools also hosting AS module exams will be hard pressed to find suitable space. Such are the pragmatic solutions which occasionally over-ride any pedagogical debate.

As the Curriculum review next shifts its focus to Advanced level provision in the school, the Head must ask what the school is doing to prepare students for the stage beyond Key Stage 5, through an Enrichment package of activities – some skills-based, such as survival cookery, first aid or car maintenance, and some more cerebral, such as philosophy or critical thinking. The school must provide a strong careers/ UCAS support system, and include curriculum time for visiting speakers, budgeting for management skills workshops or short-term specialist providers.

Somewhere in the review there should be a chance to consider what departments are doing to encourage independent study. Oddly enough, although coursework is being reduced at GCSE because of worries about plagiarism, at A level the new extended project looks set to become a part of every student's educational diet in future. Compulsory for students taking the new 14-19 Diplomas but optional for A level students, it will nevertheless be strongly encouraged through the allocation of new UCAS points. Designed to encourage independent research and individual choice of topic or theme to explore, this is one part of the national exam system which seems to be responding to the personalised learning agenda.

Just how many pupils should be in any A level set will be debated passionately by heads of department, and a new Head would be wise to reach a decision about this before agreeing innocently to some new, expensive arrangement resurrected annually forever after as a yardstick by which other departments argue their corner.

How many AS and A2 subjects a school can sensibly afford to run without losing customers to the competition is a delicate juggling act. Again, there may be mileage in investigating partnerships and collaborative initiatives, such as those 'learning pathways' in operation in maintained schools. A growing number of schools offer the IB to some, if not all, students, but it remains an expensive option where budgets are tight, and will not suit all tastes.

However, the government has voiced an intention to make the IB available in every area in the future, so it merits inclusion in a new Head's overall review of curriculum provision. A levels are destined for change, and the extended project will encourage independent study skills prior to university. Planning for such change, including budgeting for additional resources and essential staff training, should be high on every new Head's agenda.

What are the other pieces of the jigsaw? At interview, the new Head will have enthused about extra-curricular school life and emphasised a belief in a rounded education in a school providing more than an academic hothouse. So the timetable has to accommodate all those opportunities too – assemblies, PSHE, PE, games, tutor periods, rehearsal times and the like. Time allocation will be debated regularly, and key decisions will be demanded of the Head. Occasionally, they will be quite fundamental and profound – choices which draw on the core values of the school itself. The Head might have to make the final judgement, for example, on whether one period of maths in Year 9 can be sacrificed for a structured PSE programme to include drug awareness, sex education and discussions about eating disorders.

The desire to extend the curriculum to facilitate less academic experiences sometimes leads to a consideration of a two-week timetable. Supporters of this option cite its calming, less pressurising effect: opponents quote the nightmare of accommodating peripatetic staff, and the occasions when bank holidays can lead to three weeks in term-time when a particular group is not taught. And of course there are the boarding schools where teaching takes place on Saturday mornings, and where there is a need for enormous flexibility and the goodwill of academic staff to release the rowers, lacrosse teams or the 1st XV for their fixtures.

A review might identify some of these issues as worthy of wider, full-staff discussion. Certainly a full consultation period is advisable before any new Head makes changes of this type. There are always repercussions, always so many hidden details to consider, always the surprises. Heads learn the hard way that the blatantly obvious is so often not the best solution: a Head can find herself spending a disproportionate period of time meeting the needs of the peripatetic ballet teacher for Year 5, for example, simply because the only room with the sprung floor was innocently allocated as the nearest and ergo the most obvious extension of the dining room!

The next steps? Once the curriculum is agreed and implemented, the new Head should consider how she will monitor its delivery. Encouraging a culture of continuous professional development with regular reviews is where the maintained sector still leads. New Heads should check the staff development budget and ensure it is adequate to meet the school's needs. Who manages staff development? Who closes the loop by asking for feedback after a course is completed? Who evaluates the impact of the expenditure on the pupils' learning?

No amount of imaginative curriculum planning will work unless the staff are trained and confident to deliver it. A Head can install interactive whiteboards and ICT suites in every curriculum area of the school, but the will of the staff to use them all, and their training (often a hidden expense) hold greater importance. Heads of department may need training to manage the ongoing development of their staff, and to design their departmental reviews and targets to match the school's development plan.

OFSTED now expects peer evaluation of lessons, and ISI may well follow in this initiative. Again this poses a training need, and a new Head may find it useful to ask the staff development officer to conduct a skills audit to identify what training needs will be required over a few years, and then budget for them.

Inspections increasingly expect significant evidence that data is being used to influence the learning programmes. Our new Head might find it useful to be asking the deputy/director of studies how this is operated. External results may be archived for annual comparisons but what about elsewhere in the school? How is pupil progress tracked and recorded? That key question asked in state school inspections: 'How well do pupils achieve?' is a good starting point for a new Head of an independent school too.

The curriculum committee which contributed so positively and successfully to the review might now be tasked to consider other developments. Or a Head might appoint a different sub-group to review assessment, recording and reporting in the school, asking: 'How do we know if the boys and girls are underachieving – and what do we do about it? How well do departments monitor the consistency of their marking? Who decides on the schemes of work for each year group? Who is monitoring the special needs of the gifted and talented?' All these will determine the success or otherwise of the curriculum which is eventually adopted.

If a new Head is reviewing the school's information management system, consideration of the assessment management schemes currently available would be helpful. Who should manage such a system, and how will the staff use it? Assessment for learning is another area inspectors might seek to explore. Are the teaching staff aware of its merits? Is there a willing zealot who might inspire them with an in-house staff Inset?

Heads know that the most important part of their role is the appointment of effective, enthusiastic teachers. Once the curriculum needs are agreed, and once the development plan is in place, each new appointment is an opportunity to extend the staff skills base and so meet the plan's agreed targets. All candidates should be seen in the classroom context, and asked what they will add to the school's culture and community. It is often revealing to ask who or what inspired them in their own schooldays, and how they would wish to be remembered by their own pupils.

A new Head has many plates to spin, learning to meet the academic, pastoral, spiritual and social needs of the young charges in his or her care whilst remaining within the budget. But the main purpose of a school is embedded in its curriculum, and as the one who is ultimately responsible for its management, a Head has the power to open doors, introducing tomorrow's adults to concepts and competencies which will change their lives. The privilege is unparalleled.

Chapter 6

Parents

Pat Langham

'Welcome to your daughter's *At Home*.' This description of the parents' evenings was just another example of the school's quaint traditions: in 1880 the Headmistress of Wakefield Girls', Miss Allen, was *At Home* to parents between the hours of 2 and 3.30 each Tuesday – but only by pre-arranged appointment.

So was that era one of halcyon days, when parents were kept firmly in their place, and accepted the education their children were given, and were appropriately grateful? There are certainly some Heads for whom school would be a much better place if all the children were orphans or were treated as such. At least in Dotheboys Hall, Wackford Squeers could do as he wished, and never received letters of complaint about the curriculum, food or heating.

In marked contrast nowadays, many parents expect Heads to be available to them at all times, whether or not school is in session. All communication now demands an instant response, be it to a letter, an email or a phone call. The mobile phone has been described as the longest umbilical cord, and means that pupils ring home at the earliest opportunity. Often parents are in touch before anyone has time to even tell you what has happened.

Yet this should come as no surprise: education is a shared endeavour and effective education is only possible through cooperation. Parents trust us with their most precious possession and they are fully aware that their child gets only one chance. They all want the very best. They are very definitely stakeholders, and for them the stakes are high.

And so are their expectations. You must teach their children – especially the basics. Make sure they pass all their examinations, obtain a place at university, gain a degree and embark on a suitable and preferably highly paid and prestigious career – but without putting them under any pressure at all.

You are also expected to educate them in the fullest sense of the word, and that encompasses everything: to arouse an interest in music and the arts or any other talents and interests, the potential for which has not been spotted by anyone else; to keep them healthy, eating properly with nutritionally balanced meals; to be team players and to participate in sport with a balance of competitiveness and the ability to lose well; to instil in them high moral values and a solid Christian faith; to teach them all about the facts of life but to keep them away from sex, drugs, discos, and all-night parties; to teach them good manners and to make them adhere to all uniform rules; to be good citizens, possibly entrepreneurs and anything else which might become an educational imperative.

It can be an ambivalent relationship at times but the initial stages are always filled with such promise. The world is full of the people who could make the decision to send their child to your school. They are potential customers and fee payers; they are *prospective parents*.

Heads have a duty to ensure that their school is as attractive as it can be to all these parents. I know of one school which didn't even have a sign outside. Rumour had it if you were not intelligent enough to know where it was, then your children would not be intelligent enough to attend the school. From this Garbo-esque stance we all entered the Mae West School of Marketing, when it was 'Come up and see me sometime, well actually anytime'.

There are endless sources of advice on how to choose a school. Many parents have access to books which will tell them how to assess any potential school. High on the list is always a meeting with the Head. The heroic charismatic model might not be regarded as entirely appropriate any more, but as a governor once said to me when they were in the process of appointing a new Head: "When the Head walks into the room, parents need to understand why they are paying all that money".

It is at this stage that Heads have to decide what is the best personal strategy for them. Some flirt, showing themselves to be as attractive as they believe their school to be. Some are terribly approachable and sympathetic, and are often sitting in front of an open fire with a Labrador. Some adopt a magisterial distance and are rather aloof, aware that this is the stereotypical stance. Some are slightly dismissive, comfortable in the fact that they do not need the child as much as the parents want the school. Your manner, your appearance, your study and your school will all come under close scrutiny. If you pass muster, we can move to the next stage.

Your 'conversion rate' of expressions of interest to signed application forms will give a clear indication of how successful you have been. In the interim period the responsibility passes to others through the Entrance examination to results, to decisions and interviews and finally to acceptances. *Prospective* now become *new* parents and the relationship begins to develop. It is in these early stages that the ground rules are established, and you start to create the positive climate which will help effective engagement.

Communication with parents is vital, and comes in many forms. As a general rule it is advisable to tell them as much as you can, whenever you can, with a great deal of it in writing to which they can refer. This ensures that you control the information flow and the gloss you put on it. An information vacuum is soon filled by rumour and supposition, and there is real power in the playground mafia and dinner party gossip if it goes unchecked.

With regard to factual matters, compile a list of frequently asked questions, answer them all and distribute those too. Hold special evening meetings and always aim both to inform and reassure: parents who are confident in the school are less likely to worry. Communicate regularly and purposefully. The website, the magazine and newsletter are great for giving parents a real insight into the life of the school and as a source of general and specific information.

We are always very quick to contact home when a child has done wrong. However, never under-estimate the positive impact that telling parents good news or conveying congratulations will have: use planners or homework diaries to send messages, write personal letters or hand out merits. Most of our schools still have a Speech Day or Prize Giving, the most formal of the occasions, when parents are present for the public acknowledgement of their children's achievements. These are especially valuable occasions. However, there are always other opportunities to praise, and every one should be taken. Compliments must be deserved, expressions of approval genuine and heartfelt. Over-effusiveness or insincerity will have an unwished-for negative reaction.

Academic feedback is essential. Reports are closely read and analysed by every child and parent, and careful decisions sometimes need to be made about the school's approach. Will all staff be brutally honest and tell it exactly how it is? Will they be ever positive, always seeking to praise and encourage? Or will reports be realistic but carefully written, so that after pointing out a shortcoming there is a suggestion about how to improve? While staff might be writing hundreds of comments, and might sometimes wish to display their wit at the expense of a child, the parents may not be so receptive!

Almost the same conditions apply to Parents' Evenings. Being told that you have about three to five minutes with each teacher does not encourage in-depth discussion. Then there are the added frustrations of the long queues, and the garrulous parents or members of staff who far exceed their time allocation. These events must be carefully managed, with the needs of staff and parents taken into careful consideration. Alternative opportunities for more prolonged discussion should always be on offer.

Independent schools expect, and generally get, full attendance on such occasions. It is almost seen as axiomatic that our parents will be pushy, and will demand the very best for their child. The mere fact of paying implies a far greater level of involvement. We have all been faced with the 'pay your wages' approach, and we have no doubt used the common riposte of explaining that the payment gives the parent the choice of sending their child to this particular school, in order to benefit from the education provided – and that it will also allow them to pay for entry to another establishment, if they feel that is better suited to their needs.

Helicopter parents might be a recent term, vividly describing the ever-hovering, but overly protective, parents: cotton-wool-wrapped children have been with us a long, long time. It is very tempting to indulge in stereotypes. We tend too easily to forget, or even dismiss, all the supportive, cooperative and satisfied parents, while we shall always be regaled by tales of the unsupportive, the critical and the downright objectionable.

There will always be those parents who are known as difficult or as the Americans call them 'toxic': parents who expect too much of teachers and too little of their children; parents who can't accept that their children aren't perfect, whose children might be many things but 'they never lie'; parents who blame you for their children's discipline and academic problems.

Irrespective of the parental type, the way in which you deal with their concerns will determine their views of the school's effectiveness, and their levels of satisfaction with the quality of care. Tell parents at the earliest stage exactly how they are able to contact the school, and who the most appropriate person might be to help them. Encourage them to ring, no matter how trivial the issue: this reassures, and actually prevents escalation. Trivial matters can become huge if they are not dealt with as soon as possible, or if they are dismissed as trivial: a concern can soon become a complaint. Try to acknowledge phone calls or letters as soon as possible, even if it is only to tell them you will be back in touch later. This will also give you time to investigate further.

Whether a parent's concern is justified, or based on a misapprehension, or totally wrong, does not matter. Perception is more powerful than reality. If they are worried or distressed, you need to put yourselves in their shoes and aim to resolve matters. Parents must leave feeling that they were welcomed and encouraged to share their concerns with you, that they have been listened to, and where action was required that they are assured that it will happen.

There are the inevitable issues: questions about why someone else was chosen for the prize, for the concert, the lead role in the play or a place in the team; questions about why the punishment was imposed on their totally innocent child, or why only they were singled out for a uniform infringement. There will be demands to increase estimated grades for UCAS, and complaints when the child does not achieve what the parents wanted for them. There will be queries about school trips and visits, and requests to extend the already generous holiday allocation. Do not feel obliged to give in to an unreasonable request; stick by school policies and guidelines; be firm and consistent and explain why in as much detail as possible.

There will be times when the school or staff is indeed at fault or in the wrong. Admit it, apologise, explain what you will do to ensure it does not happen again, and try to do all this personally rather than in writing. When parents are completely wrong it is our job to allow them to retain their dignity. Rather than aim for a win/lose you need to ensure a win/win – otherwise you are only storing up problems for the future.

There is a predictable pattern. An instant rebuttal by the school results in parents going on an information-gathering exercise. They will contact other pupils and parents and amass as much evidence as they can to prove they are right. If they leave feeling that they were taken seriously and treated properly, you will have vocal supporters. An unhappy parent can easily become an enemy, and will do much to damage the reputation of the school.

All disciplinary matters, especially exclusions and expulsions, must be carefully managed. It is advisable to meet with the parents first, and explain exactly what you will do. Distress is inevitable, and must be mitigated. The faults of their children are not necessarily theirs, and they must believe they are working with you rather than being personally humiliated.

For those parents who become angry, or are naturally argumentative and sometimes aggressive, both you and your staff have to learn specific strategies: your normal behaviour will not be sufficient. Whether we think they are justified or not in their anger, it is important for us to treat challenging parents with the same respect as we would treat any other parent in any other situation. This involves listening carefully, and addressing only the specific issues and seeking ways forward.

If the situation does escalate, it means keeping emotions in check, choosing words carefully, looking them in the eye, and being friendly and direct. Whatever you do, do not argue, yell, use sarcasm, or behave unprofessionally with these parents – however much you may be tempted. They will have come wanting an argument, and denying it to them can be the best move. Equally important, we must remember that we are role models. It is up to us to show the most difficult parents a better way to communicate. You can always vent your frustration when they have gone!

Parents can also come in other forms. Our school has some governors who happen to be parents, but no parent representatives as such. There are obvious inherent dangers in the governor who wants to discuss catering because his child is a picky eater, or to question the curriculum because the GCSE options do not suit.

Then there are the parents who are members of the PTA: they can be the most amazingly committed workers for the school, but they can also assume superiority, believing themselves to have the ear of the Head. In extreme cases they can become a clique who believe they do run the school.

It is very much up to the individual as to whether parents become friends. There are various gradations from the formality of school social occasions, through the dinner party circuit where you are the trophy guest, to shared holidays. Parents *can* be friends – but only if no issues ever arise to do with their children and absolute confidentiality is guaranteed.

Your dealings with parents will go far beyond care for their child. Far too often nowadays a Head may be the only figure of authority who inspires respect: the one representative of continuing values of stability and respectability. As such, if you become a person whom they trust, then inevitably you will be caught up in all aspects of their lives – and you will act as marriage counsellor, mediator, social worker, financial advisor and shoulder to cry on. Dealing with the acrimony of divorced parents using their child as a pawn deserves a book in itself.

Engaging with parents is not normally a problem for independent schools, whereas some state schools struggle: the DCSF has recently introduced a Parents' Mark which rewards schools for encouraging the participation of parents and involving them in their children's learning. Other recent government initiatives have proved less welcome, such as inviting parents to share their views on an open website: an adult form of 'Rate my child's school'.

We are all now familiar with inviting parents' views for an inspection. This always tells us what we do know, and sometimes tells us things we certainly didn't know. There is great value in periodically obtaining information about the parents' likes and dislikes. This scares many staff, who believe it is an invitation to criticise. It can be an uncomfortable exercise, but it is essential if we are to be as well-informed as we should be.

We also need to match expectation to reality and it will help us to determine what wishes we can acquiesce to, and where we need to say enough and no further. While we all accept that we are accountable to parents, this must not be done in a way that undermines the authority of the school. Naturally each parent wants the best for his or her child, but individual expectations can be unreasonable and schools have a wider responsibility to provide the best possible education for all the children they serve.

Perhaps for we Heads the term *At Home* is more accurate than we might care to admit.

Chapter 7

Pastoral Care: beyond the Book and the Birch

Tim Hands

Absit omen. By coincidence, both editions of *Head to Head* have turned to the Head of The Portsmouth Grammar School for this chapter. Over the decades, PGS has not, alas, always enjoyed the best pastoral reputation. In 1805 Nelson passed the school, en route for Trafalgar and glory. Fortunately, it was on his right side. For such was the competence of the Head, Dr Forrester, then approaching his *fiftieth* year of office, that the school by then possessed no students. It was, a visiting Oxford professor recently quipped, a singularly unusual case of missing pupils on both sides.

The omen is, indeed, awkward. Has it been something about those naval traditions – "rum, sodomy and the lash," as Churchill once famously defined them? Has it been the school's historic identity as the redcoat Garrison School, with 18th century pupils dawdling on their return from lessons to watch soldiers flogged around the ramparts?

Whatever the reason, Portsmouth's authors, Dickens, Wells, Kipling (none of them, thanks to the legacy of Dr Forrester, former pupils) have all got out fast, and subsequently majored on the theme of unhappy childhood. *The Jungle Book* is but one of Kipling's fantasies on the ideal surrogate upbringing he never enjoyed. *Dombey and Son* sees the recently bereaved Mr Dombey deliver Paul to an awful boarding school run by the portly Dr Blimber. "Shall we make a man of you?" thunders Blimber. "I had rather be a child," responds Paul.

To test pastoral progress, I once used this passage as the comprehension for our Entrance interviews. "Would you like to go to a school like that?" I asked a candidate from our own Junior School. How poignantly I envied that youngster his engaging enthusiasm. Everywhere else, surely, Blimberish non-pastorality is emphatically a thing of the past. So yes, down deepest south, as the commissioning editor obviously appreciates, we need more than most to come at the fundamentals, to begin at the pastoral beginning. What exactly is pastoral care? And how and when and why did it come to be so?

It's not altogether straightforward. In my first teaching job, I remember a staff revue involving a parody of Gilbert and Sullivan's Policeman's Song. The second master, responsible for discipline, was the sergeant, and we his bobbies, mostly behind, rather than on, any beat. The theme was that the Head's pastoral reforms were eroding old style discipline, and to pupil delight we all satirically sang. This helps to place things. Pastoral care is essentially a sort of late 1970s portmanteau term – born of the thinking of the revolutionary 60s: you didn't get pastoral care in Lindsay Anderson's film *If*. To formulate your approach to it, you first need to understand the three aspects of school life historically underlying it, which I will call the disciplinary, the religious and the academic.

Discipline first. Anglo Saxon writings are pretty clear about the teacher's pastoral role: beating people. No amount of admiration for that glorious European flowering we call the Renaissance, nor any sonorous roll call of the names of its saintly educational pioneers, William of Wykeham, William of Waynflete, Harrie ye Sixte and the rest of them, should deceive us into dewy-eyed thinking that this great movement of mind altered in any way, or in any part of Europe, so essential a part of the job description of our glorious profession as the need to hit young people and hit them hard. When in the 1490s the pioneer printer Wynkyn de Worde wanted to depict a schoolmaster and pupils, he re-used a Netherlands wood cut. This showed the teacher seated on a sort of throne, large birch secure in his hand, and pupils secure and suppliant at his feet. Books are nowhere to be seen.

Ten years later, admittedly, a book had entered this revised genre piece; but also by then the birch had become longer and bushier – perhaps in response to the dissident effect of all that learning. There may always be some colleagues who believe that pastoral care and discipline are mutually exclusive, that pastoral care involves saying yes to everything. But every Head knows that the discipline is the real *sine qua non* of any school. It is the only thing which enables proper relations to flourish.

It is his responsibility and it will reflect his personality and style. There is no single right way. Too firm a touch will be counterproductive, and too light a touch will benefit no-one. Nelson punished very little; Wellington really rather a lot: yet neither exactly did a bad job in man management. Having a fixed and comfortable personal approach to disciplinary issues remains the starting point for all our communities. It constitutes the musical equivalent of tuning the orchestra, with the Head doubling (what else?) as concertmaster and principal oboe. Neglect to establish the acceptable norm, and no-one will subsequently be able to contribute properly at any point. Boundaries need establishing early: even the blind eye can never be taken off them.

Religion next. A prospective parent, shocked after visiting a boarding house, once asked a famous Roman Catholic Headmaster what his school prepared pupils for. "Madam," he allegedly responded, "of course for the grave." There is no need to ponder whether the story is true: if it isn't, there is every reason why it should be. A religious rationale has to be considered alongside the disciplinary. The origins of many of our schools are ultimately in Benedictine aspirations and lifestyles: a development of the wholer and holier person.

Often, the architecture reflects this philosophy. 'I am very happy here so far,' a new boy is supposed to have written home from King's School Canterbury, 'there is a lovely chapel in the grounds.' Modern independent schools have a wide range of religious (and non-religious) philosophies – and pupils, and Heads. But few will deny that they are looking for something more than their academic results, and the range and quality of their extracurricular activities.

For Thomas Arnold developed (and marketed) a powerful Broad Church modernisation of the Benedictine concept, which attracted Tom Brown's father, and has since attracted many, globally, into the British independent school tradition. 'Shall I tell Tom he's sent to school to make himself a good scholar?' asks Squire Brown, sturdily. 'Well, but he isn't sent to school for that – at any rate not for that mainly. If he'll only turn out a brave, helpful, truth-telling Englishman, and a gentleman, and a Christian, that's all I want.'

But suddenly it's 1979. Enter Maggie. Enter a new order. Enter league tables. If pupils like learning things, does pastoral care actually matter? To some in the 1980s it was a woolly liberalism getting in the way of the raising of academic standards, of a continuation of the social mobility which the pre-war grammar schools and post-war university grant had facilitated. "We equated the stretching of children, at all levels of ability, with caring," recalled Maggie's Education Secretary, the seminal Sir Keith Joseph – without apparent detection of any inadequacy in the statement.

I once heard a lecture on pastoral care delivered by a 1990s Government Chief Inspector which mentioned nothing but the delivery of subjects in the classroom. Yet, at the same time, all sensible Heads recognise their responsibility to fee-paying parents, and the sorts of university and employment doors that good results can open. If the results are good, there will always be an argument for saying that there is not much wrong with the school. The governors will read the league tables, attend the meeting, eat their sandwiches, and (subject perhaps only to the fillings of those sandwiches and the freshness of the bread encompassing them) return home contented.

All of this leaves the contemporary Head less with a problem than with a full scale identity crisis. The old philosophies are largely no longer there; the new ones are mostly inimical. He does not like league tables. He is not a priest. And he cannot (any more, thank goodness) hit people. He likes children, which is why he became a teacher in the first place. And he believes that teaching, surely, involves going beyond the birch.

It involves, Sir Keith, going beyond the book. It involves, my Lords,

Ladies and Gentlemen of the governing body, Madam Common Room President, Mr Common Room Secretary, and all colleagues ranged around me, some of you just in front of that blocked up doorway that formerly afforded entrance to the Common Room Smoking Room, *aiming for the heart and soul of the child.* It involves, in short, at last to use and address the term: *pastoral care.*

Pastoral care means a belief that teaching includes a commitment to pupils being happy and successful, and in that order. Pastoral care in the end involves less a set of systems than an attitude in the human heart. Pastoral care involves a certain kind of expression on the human face. "Here I see much shining wood and metal but few shining faces," the Duke of Wellington is alleged to have said, inspecting a Man of War at Devonport.

Pupils are not vessels to be filled, top down, but individuals to be got alongside, to be empathised with, to have their background understood and assisted, not just their chemistry homework graded and returned. Let the academic system produce that gleaming metalwork and woodwork – it will look particularly at home in design technology, perhaps. But the aim of the good pastoral system is shining faces. That old Duke, he knew what he was a-talking about.

On to the practicalities. What does the new Head, committed to pastoral care, need? First, I suggest, though not all readers may agree, medicine. Medical centres are the clearing house of pastoral problems, generally unacknowledged in their contribution and untapped in their potential. The majority of pastoral problems have a medical angle to them, and this is beyond the competence of the Head.

To the Medical Centre are attached not only the school doctors and nurses but also the counselling team, with the chaplain, as it were, a helpful halo on the meniscus. All time and money spent head hunting, resourcing and remunerating this team will be money well spent, and all time spent listening to it will be useful time.

They are above the Head and beyond the Head and better than the Head. They have the knowledge, they set the tone, they have the power to persuade and prescribe. Use them. Trust them and their insights into the increasing problem of pent-up adolescent anger, venting itself in ways probably unimaginable to any Head whose children have left school and graduated. More than one Head, surely, wishes he had realised their helpfulness earlier.

Parents. Mr Zephaniah has some views:

> The problem with children today
> Is their parents,
> The problem with their parents
> Was their parents,
> And their parents had big problems
> With their parents.

And so on. But it is not an easy thing, no, nor always an enjoyable thing, to be a parent. So parents also need pastoral care. Sometimes some parents may duck their own disciplinary functions, and line up with their children against the school; but, more frequently, teachers and parents too often get themselves into conflict without realising that they actually have a lot in common. Parents (like teachers) like children. They both like them to be happy. They both like them to be successful. All parents worry about their children, especially perhaps their eldest – which means that words of praise or evidence of the knowledge of the potentially unknown are usually effective beyond proportion to the quantity of praise bestowed, or sometimes (truth to tell) the quality of knowledge underlying it. *Mrs Smith: you would have been so proud had you been there this morning: I was so impressed with Nadia's response when she stubbed her toe on the bedstead.*

Settling in parents can thus be more important than settling in new pupils; and all the time which is invested in this process at an early stage will be disproportionately productive later on. Lucky therefore, those schools which have the resources to enable each family to be visited in their home by tutor or form teacher prior to the pupil taking up a place. For other schools, phone calls to home from the same staff in the early weeks are essential in establishing relationships and trust. Parents, like adolescents, actually like boundaries, and they need to know (as examples over modern attitudes to plagiarism), how those boundaries are shifting.

Parents can also be equally good at not telling you that they like boundaries – and at breaking those boundaries however carefully defined. Anyway, who said (using an unexamined plural): "Parents? I'm with my father in the holidays in leap years, Sir, and at my mother's most Sundays". The modern family is nuclear, multiple in its authority figures, and multiple in its locations. So all the more reason for guidelines on working conditions, revision programmes, Saturday jobs, unattended parties, bedtimes, boyfriends.

All these may attract ridicule in some, but they will engender respect and unspoken gratitude in the majority, and are a necessary indication of where common sense starts. They don't have to be given by you, in print, or on Speech Day. There can be information evenings on adolescence, leaflets home about GCSE revision or option choices. Be subtle, new Head, be subtle (in holiday incidents, for example, remember that you are a schoolteacher, not Chief Superintendent of Newquay). However, you will also be liked if you are bold.

Staff. Demands in day and boarding are different. To express a personal view: running a boarding house is the best training any Head can have. *The News of the World* used to claim of its pages that *All of human life is there*, and much the same could be said of a boarding house. Indeed, within the more blue chip establishments, it is sometimes possible to see the same events played out in both forums simultaneously. Being a houseparent (though perhaps not in these circumstances) is arguably the most rewarding job in education. At the same time, the demands are great, the legalities precarious, and the rationale, properly considered, undiscoverable.

The houseparent is *in loco parentis*. But Mother Nature, in her most infinite wisdom and benison, has so far not allowed even Father Science to persuade her into an extended family of 50 – and not solely on account of the latest European Working Time Directive. The houseparent has to live with these tensions; but it is ultimately the boarding Head who has somehow to manage them. In day schools, received wisdom used to be that there must either be a year or a house system, but not both. My own view has become that, given the lower staff-pupil ratios and the intensity of the shorter day, both systems are essential if the necessary checks are to be in effective operation.

Pastoral care in a day environment is actually more difficult than in boarding. To those new day school Heads seeking maximum pastoral effectiveness, I recommend a system called the Care List. Every pupil requiring in colleagues a heightened level of pastoral awareness should be on this List. It is reviewed half-termly, at a meeting chaired by the Head. Every new pupil joins the List and may not leave it until there is documented evidence of a call between home and school confirming that the pupil is now properly settled in. Generic difficulties are annually noted, and welcoming procedures thus annually improved.

The List also includes all existing pupils who have – or may have – a background pastoral problem (health, domestic, financial) and each form teacher or tutor will have agreed in advance a code describing how and at what level (*eg* counsellor, tutor, head of house, head of year, deputy head, Head) the problem is being monitored. The role of the pastoral deputy at the meeting is to ensure that all outside agencies (*eg* counsellor, Social Services) are properly considered; the role of the academic deputy is to keep an eye on any academic rank orders (*eg* half term grades). Any downward shifts of (say) greater than ten percentiles almost certainly result from – or presage – some pastoral problem.

Staff too need pastoral care. There will be happier pupils if there are happier staff. Staff development is covered elsewhere in this volume, but better common rooms, better food, better parties, better sofas, better INSET opportunities all make for happier schools. I recommend a triennial cycle of visits to another school, a different university, a different employer. Once, extending the principle, senior staff persuaded the PGS bursar to give each teacher a maximum of £50 to go anywhere they chose that would make them professionally more sunny. Shares in *Ryanair* rose. I had cards from a historian in Madrid, English teachers in Dublin, an economist in New York. I went to London. We all felt better disposed towards pupils at the end of it. Recommended.

Pupils? Well, they paradoxically belong in the section on the Head. Ignorant pupils may consider the Head their ultimate enemy; but the best Head is those pupils' most tireless defender and friend. If the job of resident house-parents is illogically multiplex in its demands, then that of a Head is more so – and hence in part the excitement, the rewards and the pleasures of the role.

To see each fixture, to answer each letter, to accept each invitation, to attend each play and sing along at each concert, to know each pupil, to remember the name of the head of biology's new husband, whose features seem remarkably similar to those of his predecessor, and yet without the lab technician (still on probation, yes?) knowingly yet having been active on them, these are amongst the immutable expectations and the certain impossibilities of Headship. Pity the poor Head who, so frequently, needs to close the study door and again contemplate whether a knotty issue requires disciplinary or pastoral treatment, or both. (And in the time of the predecessor, always remember, that door was ever ajar…)

Politics is the art of the possible, whereas Headship is merely the illusion of the impossible, effortlessly and smilingly maintained. On the one hand, the Head can no longer run the school as though it were a gigantic boarding house; on the other, the best Heads have a reputation for being everywhere and knowing everything. It can help to divide pupil contacts into the arbitrary, the regulated and the open-ended. Arbitrary contacts, that knack of being in the right place at the right time, are a matter of opportunism: all advisers concur that it is when leaning nonchalantly against a pillar on an occasional Saturday evening supper duty that the new Head's profile is seen to best and most striking advantage.

I particularly value being recommended to just the one form of open-ended contact, a Private Time each morning before school, advertised freshly each term by a handwritten note on my Board, available without appointment to pupils and pupils only. They can join the queue anonymously, bringing outstanding work for Recognition, forms to be signed, problems to mull over, distresses to share.

An intended consequence has always usefully been that no parent could ever say their child lacked an opportunity to air a concern at the highest level with the least inconvenience. Regulated contacts are an *a la carte* menu needing reconsideration each year. They can take any number of social forms (new pupil teas, weekly lunch with senior prefects or departmental staff, travelling on coaches to away fixtures or dropping in on a sports tour). Some Heads teach; mistaken Heads don't. Some sign off every UCAS form with an interview or interview every Year 11 about their future (my preference). Anyone in hospital disproportionately appreciates that impossible personal visit: but they can have a card, or the chaplain. Families in grief deserve the Head's personal attention, including a personal letter, immediately. Indeed, in general bereavement is a time when the personal lead, not least in assemblies, is essential in every regard, and can be when the salary is hardest earned.

Poor Head. Who looks after him or her? With luck, all of the foregoing parties. And let's add a special mention for that long suffering chaplain, who (if one exists, or can be found), produces, in confidence, supportive and critical views, confidential shoulders, untold pastoral benefits, and a bottle of claret that allows his halo to slip beyond its meniscus, with an accompanying exhortation that even the worst problems can sometimes appear soluble in alcohol.

The best Heads regard teaching (with its attendant ups and downs) as a vocation, but the wisest, in addition, regard logic and perspective as helpful handmaidens. The whole school development plan should be broken down into what each senior colleague will do each term. Along with a sympathetic biennial appraisal (including a questionnaire for each member of the Common Room) it forms a logical basis for subsequent evaluative reflection.

In any unexpected problem, the same sequential imperatives for discussion and debate must always prevail: what are the facts; what are the issues; what are we doing about it? If, as a Head, you haven't had a problem you feel ashamed of, astonished by, then you've either never lived – or, my son, you have lived considerably too questionably in your time prior to Headship. Have you been Head for a suicide, a murder, a rape? Have you had a current pupil convicted of armed robbery? Have members of your Sixth Form sought electronically to impersonate Barclays Bank?

All of these things have happened to Heads (and yet not one example is from a school with an Essex postcode). In every case there is a colleague with a story to share, a word of sympathy or advice to offer and a mobile number known at the headquarters of HMC in Market Harborough. Permanent exclusions can get personal, messy, knife edge (one hopes only metaphorically). The DCSF has a checklist to help Heads in the maintained sector make up their minds. Have a copy in the filing cabinet, where of course the *Exclusion* file sits next to the much fatter *Excursion* file, which serendipitously houses your holiday brochures.

Ah yes, holidays. And hobbies. And husbands, and wives, and children, and all those passions and recreations and escape routes that allow you to give pastoral care to yourself. Yes, Headmaster, even amongst your many responsibilities, including those to your family, that golden pastoral rule applies even to you: *you* must be happy also, or how can your school be? These opportunities and obligations and pleasures and delights do more than help. These opportunities must be logically and dispassionately planned.

So, rejoice, Williams both. Rejoice, King Henry ye sixte. Education has travelled much over the years. Why, it even, in 1732, arrived in Portsmouth, when Dr William Smith decided to start Portsmouth's first school. And it came back there, in imagination anyway, on or around 1 October 1838, when Nicholas Nickleby stirred revolution in Yorkshire at Dotheboys Hall, and overturned Wackford's desk and – yes, Wynkyn, can you imagine it? – actually beat the Headmaster and fled the premises.

I read that passage to parents with growing gusto each year, as though lulled back into some Anglo-Saxon time warp. They begin to shift uneasily in their securely bolted seats. Is this really the school where the inspectors concluded that pastoral care, formerly a significant weakness, was now a particular strength? Tempted, I up the inflections as the narrative roars to its educationally anarchic conclusion and Nicholas flogs Wackford to within inches of his life.

For every Head must live with a firm sense of original sin. Every Head must acknowledge weakness. Every good Head must recall his own adolescence, and live through it in his head again, because (like everyone else) he will have razed it, in all its awfulness, from the memory. Every Head must remember the wise words spoken in *Measure for Measure* to the icy deputy, Angelo, by an oddly named Viennese clown: "Does your worship mean to geld and splay all the youth of the city?"

Reader, for *Head to Head*, now read *Eyeball to Eyeball* – the governing metaphor perhaps, of this essay. The life of the Head, entrusted with pastoral care, is a life of tension. Being a Head means being a friend to the young, a shepherd of their parents, and a leader respected by one's colleagues. It is a difficult but a wonderful life. Too blind an eye, Dr Forrester, may result in missing pupils on both sides. Too firm a hand, Mr Squeers, and you may alienate Nicholas and Smike (who ended, of course, their journey in Portsmouth). Too little humanity or too much licence and you will end up with the conflicts that rip apart the world of both young and old in *Measure for Measure*. *Absit omen*? That Viennese clown's odd name, Pompey, strikes home as an uneasy reminder that all pastoral roads lead towards and commence with the tensions in one's own back yard.

How will it all end? Consider retirement, Headmaster (though alas this book contains no chapter on it). The grandchildren, the slippers on the hearth, the story books. In particular that story book by the benevolent clergyman (who saw so clearly into human hearts that he became a multi-millionaire) which contains a tale entitled *Saved from Scrap*, a fable of Trevor the Traction Engine. Worn out, Trevor was to be sold for scrap, but his kindly heart and kindly deeds engaged the sympathy of those who knew the good turns he had done for the young, and he was rescued and revered and placed in retirement within the symbolic location of an orchard, where he could watch the young play around him.

He was happy. 'Long afterwards' the author tells us, 'you will see him shut his eyes, remembering. "I like children," he whispers happily.' Out of the mouths of babes and traction engines comes this real and rewarding and final message of pastoral care, and this summary of the pleasures and privileges of the vocation that is entrusted with it.

Once, presumably, a puff of smoke from a Roman chimney greeted St Gregory, paragon of Popes, prior to his becoming biographer of St Benedict. Latterly, and more frequently, a puff of smoke from behind a corrugated iron bike shed has marked in many a school the onset of adolescent experience. But always, for the Head interested in pastoral care, at times of tension and at times of contentment, this peaceful and triumphant puff of Trevor's white smoke brings reassurance and affirmation, and a reminder of all the rewards.

Chapter 8

Finance

David Hempsall

"Why me, guv?" Perhaps I should begin by setting out what might be regarded as my *bona fides*. At the time of writing, I am in my twenty-second and final year of Headship. I've had the privilege of leading two, very different, schools. In neither were we so flush with cash that we could afford to be anything but careful, a situation which will resonate with a large majority of Heads. My awareness of financial constraints has curbed any inclination I may have had towards extravagance of thought or deed.

As it is, my own tendencies are Calvinist. As a head of department, it was a matter of principle that, at the end of the year, I would bring my expenditure in exactly on budget. As a consequence, my submissions were invariably accepted without demur, even when they included a modest increase. At the opposite end of my career, I have for the last six years been HMC's treasurer. In this role, through a mixture of good luck and reasonable judgement, I've been fortunate to enjoy a bit of success, helping HMC to fulfil a long-standing, strategic objective in purchasing its own headquarters in Market Harborough, leaving the Conference beholden to no-one. Hence the assumption is abroad that I know a bit about finance.

In truth, I have taken on roles in which money happens to have figured very prominently. In each, the learning curve has been extremely steep. Nowhere was this truer than when, in a previous life, I was vice-chairman of an NHS Trust, handling an annual budget in excess of £43,000,000. I shall remember for the rest of my life signing a seven-figure cheque for one particular building project.

In all the roles I have taken – and that includes being a Head – I have been careful with the money. Why? Because it isn't mine. How have I learned what I've learnt? Because I've had to. It's certainly not been through any form of training. Like most Heads, I suspect, I am largely self-taught: the archetypal kinaesthetic learner!

In that regard too, I belong to a generation of Heads who experienced the last recession. There are many – perhaps now a majority – who have no experience at all of any significant economic down-turn and it's a genuine concern that those not so schooled will be left bereft when the next recession occurs – as occur, it will.

Money makes the world go around, according to Sally Bowles. It doesn't, of course, but it – or rather a lack of it – can certainly bring your bit of the world grinding to a halt. So what can – or perhaps should – any Head do, to try to ensure that the cogs mesh rather than screech? There are, I think, three aspects to be considered. They are technical, relational and moral which, perversely, I shall consider in reverse order.

The business of education in which we are all engaged is, at root, a moral enterprise; so let's begin with the morality. Before anyone reaches for the shotgun, let's address some basic financial realities. In most schools, there are two sources of income. The first is endowment, if you're lucky! The second is fees. In most schools this is the principal revenue stream; in many, it's the sole such source.

In the two schools in which I've had the privilege of being Head, we had a culture in which talking about "the school's money" was *verboten*. Rather it was a self-denying ordinance. We talked instead of "parents' money", cash which was (usually very) hard-earned. Appreciating that fact imposed an imperative: that was to spend the money wisely, directing as much of it as possible at the school's core activities of teaching and learning. That is why, to this day, I remain frankly sceptical about additional calls on that money which emanate from agencies beyond the Head's control.

When setting the annual subscription level for HMC membership, I always applied a rough rule of thumb. Neither of my two schools was flush with money but if my annual membership of HMC cost the school the equivalent of the tuition fees of one child for one term, I'd regard that as acceptable, given the service I received from the Conference. Unscientific it may be; but the formula has a kind of logic. The fact remains that payment of that subscription, whatever it may have been and however marginally, detracted from my ability as Head to allow colleagues to deliver what they were employed to do: teaching.

At times, I do wonder whether other organisations in the sector – AGBIS, ISC, ISI and the like – ask themselves the same questions and appreciate that, in requiring subscription payment, it is parents' money that they are taking from schools. Providing good value for money is and always has been an issue. It is one which, in the years to come, will assume an increasing significance for our sector.

From the macro- to the micro-moral, let me offer some advice which, whilst it may well be utterly superfluous, won't stop me giving it anyway. Generally speaking, Heads these days are paid decent salaries. Stories are legion of Heads who once lived the life of Reilly at the school's expense. I suspect that those days are gone, as one of the genuinely good things to emerge from the culture of accountability is the assumption that expenditure necessarily incurred on school business will be modest.

Whilst paying to travel on the West Coast line may still involve mortgaging the inheritance, there are relatively inexpensive options to be considered. For my part, I never thought I would live to see the day when those behind the *guichet* at a railway station would utter the words: "The best deal I can do for you is..." Hallelujah! The notion of service is not yet dead.

In our trade, it is absolutely essential that we practise what we preach. Particularly when circumstances are straitened, we urge colleagues towards sensible economy. Nothing erodes confidence more quickly than the suspicion – no matter how ill-founded – that the Head is living on the hog. It is essential to be one hundred per cent scrupulous.

I turn next to the relational aspects of finance. Mutual trust is the *sine qua non* of Head-governor relationships. It is the role of the governor to be the Head's critical friend. Having appointed the chief executive, governors must trust the Head at every turn and in no area more than determining how the incoming resources are to be expended. In that regard, there are key personnel on whom the Head too has to rely.

First, in presenting a budget to governors, the Head is dependent upon heads of department who put together their requests. In my experience, there is discussion and some negotiation before what is agreed is aggregated for submission to the governors for approval. I take it that this is quite a common model. The 'top-down' approach seems no longer to be in vogue, rightly a victim of the more consultative and collaborative approach which prevails these days.

Now, of course, departmental budgets are small beer when set alongside salaries, bursaries, capital projects and the gaping maw which is ICT. Nonetheless, what's spent on the day-to-day delivery of the core business is very important in setting a tone, reconciling financial expectation and realism.

In dealing with heads of department, I would recommend two complementary approaches. The first is what I rather unimaginatively call 'zero budgeting'. In almost every organisation in which I have worked, budgeting generally proceeded on a historical basis. We all know the formula. What did we do last year? Let's add a bit for inflation. Any big items and/or projects? Stick 'em in and, hey presto! We arrive at a budget.

This is lazy and, of course, is also the way that government operates. The budgetary process has to be much more rigorous than this. There can be no sacred cows. This is why I advocate the 'zero budgeting' approach. Simply put, it means that every year, each and every head of department has to build up his or her bid from a base of absolutely nothing. In this way, colleagues themselves think very, very hard indeed about just what it is that they need to deliver their part of the school's core activities. For my part, in discussion with the bursar, I have a pretty clear idea in advance of meeting heads of department just what may be the global sum that we will have to assign to teaching and learning.

I would also urge in the strongest possible terms that those discussions which lead to the fixing of each departmental budget should involve only two people, namely the Head and the head of department: no-one else. In some schools, bursars are involved but, with the greatest respect, it is the

Head - and only the Head – who can discriminate between competing educational claims.

Those bursars with whom I have worked have, to a man, been delighted to operate in this way. It's the Head's responsibility to make the difficult – and sometimes unpopular – decisions; it's the bursar's to administer the outcomes. In my experience, this *modus operandi* has led to relationships between the bursar and heads of department being extremely cordial.

The second approach is one which, whilst the general principle can be universally applied, requires local interpretation. In my situation, I work on a triennial cycle which results in the aggregate departmental budget being roughly the same year on year. Let me explain. It's a truism that there are departments which, in relative terms, are expensive. ICT is unique, of course. It is a black hole. Chemists necessarily pour down the sink sums of money which could fuel entire humanities faculties. That is simply the way it is.

As Heads, we recognise a pattern in departmental expenditure. In Year 1, in addition to the routine expenditures, there is heavy capital development. In Year 2, the head of department and colleagues realise what they forgot to include in the capital programme implemented in Year 1 and seek to 'top up'. In Year 3, things go quiet through a mixture of embarrassment and satisfaction. Then the cycle begins all over again.

It's my recommendation that, by studying departmental expenditure very carefully, the Head should phase Years 1-3 developments over that three-year period so as to keep overall expenditure across departments roughly level. It means, of course, that different subject areas are at different stages of the three-year cycle at any one time, but I have found that by being entirely frank with heads of department, they have fallen in with this approach very willingly indeed; they know that, surely as night follows day, their turn will come. The exception is ICT: if anyone has an answer, then either (a) answers on a post card, or (b) become a consultant and make a fortune.

I alluded earlier to the relationship between Head and bursar. Anecdotes are legion about this particular relationship and they usually involve conflict. As a Head, I have worked with three bursars, all of whom acted also as clerk to the governors. On the management chart, amidst all the solid lines of command, there was the sinister, dotted line running directly from the bursar to the board of governors.

Never once has this constitutional arrangement given me cause for concern. All three of my bursar colleagues used a similar analogy. If the Head is the chief executive officer, then the bursar is the finance director. In the event of there being conflict, then it is the finance director who has to go. Happily, that situation has never arisen. All three bursars were – and are – their own men. We would have our disagreements. In argument, each of us would win some and lose some. At the end, we would arrive at a solution which we believed was in the best interests of the school. We remained the best of colleagues and friends.

Indeed, for the school to succeed as a business, Head and bursar must be joined at the hip. Almost every decision the Head takes will have a financial implication and wherever possible, the Head must discuss what has to be resolved with his senior colleagues – and especially the bursar – to ensure that whatever decision is reached has been fully tested. This approach has the collateral benefit of engaging the bursar in academic and educational issues.

If stories about bursars are legion, so too are those about Heads who, thinking themselves above the grubby realities of money, have taken decisions without any consultation, leaving the bursar to try to clear up the consequences. Whatever the flow charts may show, the Head-bursar relationship must be based on absolute and mutual trust. Simply put, I can't do my job if the bursar doesn't do his; and *vice versa*.

This draws me on to my third category, the technical aspects of finance and relates to the previous point about the symbiotic nature of the Head-bursar relationship. I wrote earlier that I am a kinaesthetic learner. I have had to be. When it came to money, Heads have an obligation – yes, an obligation – to achieve a certain level of financial literacy. Simply put, if a Head can't read and understand a balance sheet or management accounts, he or she should learn. This is a basic skill which is not difficult to master. Ignorance is not an excuse. It is entirely reasonable for the bursar to expect his or her CEO to have a grasp of data which are the common currency of management.

By the same token, bursars and accountant governors are not averse to common sense being brought to bear on their arcane science. I've learnt that nothing is set in concrete. In four organisations in which I've been heavily involved, I found myself at a loss as those leading the discussion have darted around the balance sheet. I summoned the courage to ask that, in future, items be tabulated down the left-hand side in alphabetical order. On all four occasions, I detected a sympathetic sigh of endorsement from other lay members. It's been frankly amazing to find just how much time has been saved by making this tiny adjustment to procedures.

Lest it be thought that finance should cause the Head to lose the sense of vision, far from it! Financial management involves knowledge, judgement and a lot of common sense. Equally, it is right sometimes – sometimes often – to think the unthinkable. It's no bad thing to turn the glass upside down from time to time.

This is absolutely crucial when it comes to considering and then implementing strategic change, be it in building or curriculum or staffing. I well remember two especially enthusiastic young members of staff coming to see me six months into my second Headship. They were both keen to introduce a new A level subject and one which I'm sure they knew had been taught with conspicuous success in my previous school.

In they polled to make their case. Between them, they said, they would need only eight periods a week, then the standard, in-house allocation for an A level subject in a 40-period week. "In the first year," I rejoindered; "and the same in the second year means we're talking about half a member of staff." "And what," I asked, "about the start up and then the running costs? What about accommodation, books, equipment and technical support? Is there any evidence of a demand for this subject?" Their crestfallen expressions told me that they'd thought I'd be a push-over. They were sent on their way with an instruction to put together a proper business case. They did; the subject was introduced 18 months later, and very successfully too.

The moral of the tale is two-fold. First, there is the importance of detailed forward planning with appropriate – for which read realistic – lead times. Secondly, there is the general proposition which is that Heads who operate an open-door policy may have to listen to 100 ideas, of which 98 are pretty well useless. The skill lies in identifying the two ideas which, if panned and sieved, will prove to be pure gold.

I referred earlier to the last recession. People were pulling in their horns. After long and careful discussions with those who were my governors at the time, we resolved to do precisely the opposite of what passed for conventional wisdom. We decided to spend when the indicators said save, just as we'd saved against future difficulty when things had been relatively easy and everyone else appeared to be spending hand over fist.

The logic of this was undeniable. During the last recession, the cost of construction dropped like a stone. The price of steel was more than halved. Having hoarded our pennies, we were able to build inexpensively in the depths of a recession when contractors were prepared to build barely above cost simply to help the cash flow, retain their work force and keep in business. It's the same logic which says: plan for a down-turn when things are on the up. It matters not one jot whether you believe in seven- or 13-year cycles: to borrow the metaphor which economists have half-inched from the physicists, what goes up comes down.

From this, it will be clear that sometimes there is merit in perversity. There have been many, many occasions too when I have acted contrary to my own instincts by spending money. I remember very well one of the first pieces of advice I was given by a very senior and academically-minded Head. "If ever you have money left over and can't think what to do with it," he said, "spend it on paint." It was sound advice.

It's a genuine privilege to visit other schools wearing my ISI hat, but my heart has sunk on several occasions when I've seen premises which would have been improved immeasurably by a lick of paint. At my own school, it is part of the after-school Friday ritual that Tom the Painter goes around, making good the scuff marks which are an inevitable by-product of having 800 lively pupils on site. As a result, the plant always looks spick and span.

Indeed, it's often the routine which gets overlooked in the competition for finite resources. Tired classroom and office furniture impresses no-one, least of all visiting parents. The training budget is often one of the first to suffer when there's a financial draught. Whilst Heads are generally very good at encouraging other colleagues to go on courses, few are quite so good at attending to their own professional development: not too many physicians healing themselves, I fear.

From the visionary to the bread-and-butter – and here wc have come full circle. One of the most difficult exercises in which Heads are involved lies in contributing to the annual discussion about setting fee levels. In what has always been, *pace* the Office of Fair Trading, a competitive market, there are a number of elements which are easy to factor in.

In most schools, for example, staff salaries account for about two-thirds of annual expenditure. In many, the annual pay settlement in the maintained sector is a weighing factor. Then there are school-specific allowances to be added. There are some recurrent and reliable pointers to the level at which fees should be fixed.

Then we come to the imponderables on which some governors can become horribly hooked. These include inflation, however that may be calculated; the Retail Prices Index, whatever that is and however it may be produced. There are any number of official and unofficial indices. Ultimately, however, the determinant will be just what the local market will bear. Governors, especially the commercially-minded, will demand hard evidence of just what that is and, of course, there is almost none.

There will be some indicators: numbers of parents defaulting on fees or applying for bursaries, for example. Knowledge of local demographics and competitors' published fees will be helpful. Even with all these clues, however, the case will hang very largely on the Head's experience of, and feel for, local factors. When all comes to all, it is a matter of judgement. My advice on this is to be bold.

Why? It is a truism in commerce that more businesses go to the wall through under-charging than for over-charging for a quality product. I've always been more bullish than governors on fees. In retrospect, I should have been even more forceful in arguing my case for, in 22 years of Headship, I've received only two letters querying fee increases, and not a single child has ever been withdrawn as a result. Parents are not fooled by government statistics: they are very inflation-savvy. As ever, it is important to take the medium-term view: when setting fees, it is not the rate for next year but the platform for the year after that which really matters.

So we arrive where we set out. In an era when phrases like 'charitable activity' and 'public benefit' will become part of the *lingua franca*, the fact remains that our schools have to be run on sound, business-like lines. That is a legal requirement. If they are not, there will be neither charity to dispense, nor benefit to confer.

As a Mancunian, a liberal and a *Guardian* reader *passé*, my view of the independent sector is pragmatic and, to those of a more conservative persuasion, close to heretical. There shouldn't be a need for an independent sector. The fact is that despite the billions poured into the maintained sector, the need for independent schools is as great as ever.

Having been politically marginalised and even defensive for a generation, the sector has re-gained confidence in itself; and not a moment too soon. Provided we hold to the vision of a liberal education – however that may be interpreted in our individual schools – and observe financial good practice in translating vision into the everyday experience of the children in our care, the contribution we make to Education UK plc and the influence we wield will become even more disproportionate.

Chapter 9

Boarding

Hilary Moriarty

Your phone rings at midnight, and an irate parent demands to know what you intend to do about the row her daughter is having – right now this minute – with a member of staff. You say, "I will deal with this in the morning, it is now midnight!", and the parent says, "You are my daughter's headmistress, and if I feel like phoning you at two o'clock in the morning, I will do so!"

That's when you really know you are Head of a boarding school and there is no place to run. The above event actually happened during my Headship: the girl and the member of staff were on a personal development course, team-building, bonding and camping in the school grounds for two nights. The parents were in Africa, with all that entailed in terms of time differences. And the girl had fallen out with the member of staff in a dispute over whether said pupil was ill enough to be sent back to school. Stroppy teenager phones home, parents believe only the Head can fix it, so they call. It doesn't happen often, but you don't forget when it does.

Rule 1: Be very careful to whom you give your telephone number.

You might ask, 'How did the parent's problem get straight to the Head? Were there not layers of management through which the parents would have to work before they got to the top?' The answer to that is, 'Yes, but…' These parents really believed only the Head would do. It was the middle of the night; their daughter had clashed with a senior member of staff. For the daughter to get what she wanted (to stay in the tent even if she was ill), only the Head could over-ride the member of staff's decision to send her in.

The situation most likely to take parents straight to the Head is a clash between pupil and teacher. For most other things, they will accept the published chain of command, from teacher to form teacher to head of year to head of pastoral care or curriculum, to deputy head. But if the judgement of a member of staff is being called in to question, they are likely to go straight to the top. The Head will pay a price if she over-rides a teacher, but for the parent, that is the Head's problem.

The opportunities for clashes between pupils and members of staff are, I believe, far more in a boarding school than in a day school. A boarding pupil works with academic staff in the daytime, and (possibly) a whole different group of people between 4pm in the evening and 8am in the morning. Moreover, pupils are far more likely to consider these hours belong to them – as they would if they attended a day school. Hence any control or prohibition will be felt the more keenly because it appears to intrude upon 'their time', when what they would really like to do is very different from what the school expects or what parents think they have bought into, by sending their child to board.

And the Head at the end of a phone day and night if they need you, is probably part of what every parent believes they have bought into. The Head is part of the package. Most parents intend never to call the Head out of hours; very few ever do it. But they have trusted you with the most precious thing in their world: their child. You are responsible, and you stand accountable for every element of that child's life while they are within your gates.

It is a truly awesome responsibility, and part of the proof we offer to parents that we do take it seriously is to be available 24 hours a day. You sincerely wish for nothing to go wrong which could call you from your bed, but you should be ready for it – and pleased if you are able to rise to the occasion, whatever its demands. Parents will speak well of you if you do, and you will take a quiet pride in having been at your post when the bullets flew.

Remember that it is not for nothing the job very often comes with on-site accommodation. There is much to be said for retaining a bolthole elsewhere, though a small hotel will suffice in emergency, and you may be lucky to get to either in term time.

Rule 2: Be prepared for a boarding headship to be 24 hours a day.

The next major difference between a boarding headship and leading a day school is that it's a seven-day-a-week job. Boarding schools have increasingly tried to accommodate the demands of the market by offering weekly and flexible boarding, as well as full boarding. Whatever the mix in your school, if there are boarders on the premises at weekends, you're still in charge.

Most boarding schools will work out a rota for the term with other staff taking turns at being the duty person for some of the weekends. The reality is that if something goes wrong, the Head will be called. And that's exactly what you would want. What you don't want is to return on Monday morning to find a full boarder has been arrested for shop-lifting or there was a minor accident with the minibus taking pupils to a rugby match, "But thcy're fine now, Boss!" Hence the Head being off duty is never quite as possible as it looks, and, as with being available around the clock, perversely this is exactly as you would wish.

Weekends at boarding school can (and should) be very full. Some will teach on Saturday mornings (with a complicated impact upon academic timetables, giving people half days in lieu all over the week); even if they don't, there will be matches. One boarding Head of my acquaintance came in for heavy flak from pupils and parents because he would attend musical evening events but never made it to the games field. They thought he demonstrated how unimportant sport was in his world, and therefore his school. It bred deep resentment.

So be prepared to be even-handed in your support of all your pupils do. Keep a diary for proof. Be visible in all places, clapping or yelling as the case may be, or singing, reading, praying or preaching in the Sunday chapel services which are almost always part of the boarding school weekend. And then there's Sunday evening, when boarders who have been away for the weekend return. Ideally, you'll be in the Hall, ready to greet them, see parents if only briefly, catch any problems on the hoof, make both pupils and parents feel at home. Cue for blazing fire in winter, jugs full of flowers in the summer, tea and biscuits in all seasons for those with a long drive back.

The good boarding Head is always, always, taking the chance to talk to parents, to remember their names and their child's recent successes, to ask how the dog is, if the last time you saw them, the dog was having surgery.

You can ask for such commitment from your staff, but it's not easy to generate, (and if you find it, promote the member of staff in question). However, the best way is to demonstrate it yourself. Lovely when you chat to a parent and a member of staff later says, "I didn't know her grandmother had just done a world cruise – how do you remember all that?" The answer is because you are the face of the prospectus, in which every school declares, 'Your child is an individual, and he/she really matters to us'. You can show that the child really matters to you. It is probably absolutely true, but the good boarding Head demonstrates it. Then parents who only hope it's true can believe it.

Rule 3: Be prepared to work seven days a week, every week.

Since it's going to tie you to your post day and night, and will probably do more than double your workload, be clear about how you want the boarding half of your world to look and feel and operate. If it is not the way you would like it, you'll be helpless when a parent or pupil complains about the way it is, and you agree with them.

Review all policies to do with boarding as soon as you land the job. Some may be archaic, and the world does indeed change. One experienced boarding Head speaks of discovering, with a shame-faced smoker standing in front of him, that the school's policy required a month's suspension for a first smoking offence. Bad enough to have to enforce a tough policy; worse if you don't actually agree with it.

Be sure that you're happy with what you find, and that any actionyou have to take accords with what you genuinely believe to be The Right Thing To Do. When things go wrong, the policies you have will be the ones by which you will be judged: did you do what the policies said you would do if whatever happened?

Similarly, make sure the policies are known by the school and parent community. If a pupil transgresses, and knew in advance what the penalty would be, he has less defence than one who had no idea he could be asked to leave for that particular misdemeanour. This will be true in all schools, but the boarding Head has to be alert to the increased possibilities for transgression that will occur when pupils are out of the classroom – cyber bullying in the IT room, smoking in the tree house, drinking in the common room, taking drugs in the cricket pavilion, having sex in a deserted dorm. (Are you *still* sure that you want the job?)

Many of these crimes and misdemeanours will be exactly what their mates are doing in the evenings and at weekends if they happen to attend day schools. Many boarding pupils are actually sent to a boarding school in the first place because their parents want to protect them from a modern world which seems to rob them of a decent childhood and push them into an adolescence riddled with risk. The young people themselves may not quite see it like that.

Increasingly, as more schools become co-ed, a school will need clear policies about sex between pupils. If popular statistics are right, up to 60% of 16 year-olds have been in sexual relationships. How will your school respond if it happens on your watch? Remember that sex with a person younger than 16 is a criminal offence, and must be reported to Social Services for investigation.

Many policies, when it comes to penalties, contain words such as 'may', or 'at the Head's discretion'. While these are understandable *caveats* allowing the Head to react to particular circumstances as he deems fit, there is also something to be said for clarity and certainty. When it comes to crime and punishment, pupils and parents alike are likely to want fairness and transparency. It cannot be good policy to ask for the removal of one pupil who has been a pain since he arrived, but to turn a blind eye to the behaviour of another who is the star of the rugby team, and who is only six weeks away from probably excellent A level exams.

One last word on policies: remember that while the Head may devise them and enact them, child protection policies belong to the governing body, which must review them and the school's performance in this area every year.

Rule 4: Own your policies, make sure they are known.

In less alarming times, stay in close touch with how boarding is going on a daily basis. It goes without saying that there should be regular meetings with boarding staff, but they can be incredibly difficult to arrange, given the complications of house staff time off. House staff will also keep records of the days, (and nights), which the Head should see, and in which he should take a genuine interest. Listen to pupils: there should be a forum of some kind through which you hear from pupils about what they like and what they don't. If you don't know, how can you continue to improve your school's provision for boarders?

Be an occasional, even frequent, presence. There are many ways to organise this – dinners with year groups, coffee with houses, dropping in to several houses an evening, dropping in at prep or during activities, watching television, at bedtime, after lights out, at mealtimes – even breakfast. It's important that staff should feel your presence as supportive, not snooping, and that pupils should see you as knowing a bit more about their boarding lives than you would have done if you had stayed in your remote office or cosy home.

Judging the Best Decorated Dorm at Christmas, or buying up all that's left over after a Young Enterprise sale, are the easy bits. It's a brave Head who takes part in an end of term Karaoke evening or abseils with the boarders for Red Nose Day, but they are all part and parcel of the all-round life of a boarding school.

Increasingly, inspectors of all kinds in schools are asking not just: 'What does a school do?' but also: 'How do you know it's working?' Regular surveying of pupils (and parents) is a good idea, in addition to a complaints box. Then, when inspectors do arrive, you can depend upon the responses from pupils when they talk to them and on replies to questionnaires far more than would have been the case a few years ago.

At the time of writing, the Head and all boarding staff should know both the 52 Minimum Standards for Boarding Schools, upon which boarding inspections have been conducted by the Commission for Social

Care Inspection for some years, and the details of the five outcomes of 'Every Child Matters', which will be paramount in inspections to be conducted by Ofsted from April 2007.

Boarding inspections will take place every three years, but with annual self-evaluation to keep schools on their toes. There is certainly a move towards schools having little or no notice – down eventually perhaps to inspectors arriving within two days. Therefore having all the paperwork in order and in the right place and easily accessible, even if the inspectors are coming when it's time off for the head of boarding, is vital. In fact, it's probably worth instigating occasional 'inspector drills', in the same way as a fire drill. What would happen if staff were told today that a team of inspectors was arriving in 48 hours? Become your own inspector – or borrow a kindly local Head to act the part – and see how you fare against the five outcomes/52 standards.

Boarding inspection reports are published; they provide for parents a useful guide to schools. Here is the external judgement of how a school performs in all manner of areas, regardless of what it says about itself in its prospectus or website. Inspectors will be looking for constant improvement, so expect the bars to go up every time you're inspected. A Head recently reported that at his last inspection, his risk assessment for a boarding house was perfectly acceptable. The next time inspectors came, they wanted a separate risk assessment for each boarding house – perfectly reasonable if there were any differences at all between the houses, or the ages of pupils within them, and an indication of how the stakes had been raised between inspections.

Rule 5: Really know your boarding, warts and all. If you're finding warts, fix them.

Staffing your boarding may be the most important thing you can do to make a difference to a boarder's life. You may know exactly what you would like in boarding staff, but it can be very difficult to find, and it is likely to become increasingly expensive.

Much will depend upon the character of boarding in the school you join. Some are large schools with small boarding numbers. Schools where the population is all boarding are increasingly rare, but many have a population which is half boarding, half day. Some have separate boarding houses, often housing boarders of all years; others have large buildings divided, for instance, by floor, for different year groups.

House staff can be equally varied: some teach, some do not. Some schools have academic staff drafted in to supervise prep, organise evening activities, and to plan and run whole Saturdays and Sundays. This can lead academic day staff to wonder what the house staff are for, but such spreading of the load of the seven-days-a-week responsibility for pupils' welfare and happiness can be a vital part of making both academic and boarding staff feel part of the same school, rather than two halves of the same school, uneasily separated by the four o'clock bell.

Whatever the pattern of your boarding, be alert to the strains and stresses upon boarding staff, who may be teaching all day and supervising lively and demanding youngsters until 11pm. They are much harder to replace than academic staff, because pupils build relationships with them over and beyond the simply professional teacher-pupil contract, and parents get to know them as friends too. House staff have more daily contact with their child than does the Head, however great you are at your job. So house staff are worth looking after, not least in the matter of working time.

Boarding schools depend for their daily lives upon boarding staff not being clock-watching individuals who will leave on the dot of their official time off, regardless of whether their replacement has arrived. The best are well aware of the demands of the job before they take it on. But these days, Heads and governors are more responsible than ever for the well-being of their staff. Ensuring the health and well-being of house staff will never be easy, whilst also ensuring that pupils are as well looked after as parents wish, by staff whom they know, trust and expect to be always there; meeting that challenge is all part of the boarding Head's job.

Rule 6: Look after your boarding staff.

House staff who live on site may well be adversely affected by the kind of holiday letting which most boarding schools now organise for their premises, to capitalise on their prime resource: the buildings and site. Some schools designate a time in the holidays when there will be no lettings. This is obviously a useful time for maintenance work, but even that can be noisy and even disruptive.

The lettings programmes are usually vital to a school's financial operation, so you may be able to do little about them, but it is worth considering the impact upon house staff at the planning stage, particularly if a letting runs close to the start of term, with a knock-on effect on readiness for the pupils' return. It is also worth being very clear about your own responsibilities for any holiday lettings programme, or you may find the job is also 365 days a year.

Rule 7: Remember that the Head as well as the house staff needs holidays.

The responsibilities of a boarding Head are the most you can ever expect in a Headship: for obvious reasons, no day school can compare with it. A boarding school is the most complex of schools, and the most delicate of mechanisms, subject to the vagaries of the market places for full, weekly and flexi-boarders, to the demands of pupils as young as seven and as old as 19, male and female and from all over the world as well as Britain. It often needs to juggle the requirements for these pupils with those of a day population of pupils who must feel equally important. At the end of the teaching day, an army of staff will move in to cover the non-teaching day, with their own hopes and dreams, aspirations and difficulties.

Headship of such an organisation is the most demanding job in education today. It's also the most fulfilling, the most rewarding, the most worthwhile. Bring to it your experience, your energy, your enthusiasm.

Rule 8: Above everything else, enjoy it.

Chapter 10

Development and Fundraising

Priscilla Chadwick

First contacts with the world of *development* can be confusing and disorientating. Heads have traditionally focused on strategic development planning in relation to curricular, pastoral or financial matters; they have devised departmental or school development plans at all levels; they have consulted with governors to ensure that the development of new facilities enables the school to keep up-to-date. Just when they think they have mastered all development issues, along comes another, very different concept of the word.

Welcome to the world of fundraising, friendraising, annual giving, 'high net-worth individuals', philanthropy and 'invested constituents'. The USA has had years of practice and experience in alumni-nurturing and alumni-giving: the Ivy League universities raise millions of dollars every year to resource scholarships and professorships, and British universities have in recent years introduced long-term fundraising programmes on a similar model investing significantly in 'development': Cambridge for example has set the target of raising £1billion by 2012.

Development and marketing are sometimes closely linked, as the two roles have issues in common: without a culture of successful recruitment, fundraising initiatives may struggle to make any impact. Few schools can afford not to 'market' themselves: after all, pupil numbers have the most direct impact on a school's cash-flow. But educationists are often slow to realise the importance of 'selling' the school to potential customers beyond creating that glossy prospectus, welcoming Open Days and achieving top league table examination results.

Over-subscribed independent schools with long waiting lists and significant endowments may feel somewhat complacent, but any downturn pressures in the economy can quickly change that. The vast majority of fee-paying schools and, increasingly, state schools in particular areas, need to market their achievements and nurture their reputation through word-of-mouth and good media coverage, thus preparing the ground for potential development and fundraising.

The legal requirement on fee-paying schools to provide evidence of 'public benefit' to justify their charitable status has focused the minds of governors and Heads on the need particularly to increase bursaries and scholarships, in order to fund free or subsidised places for deserving children. Generating sufficient funds from annual surpluses, in effect paid for by current parents' fees, is probably unrealistic for most schools, so the pressure is on to tap into that same alumni/ae market which higher education has shown can be responsive to such appeals. The constant demand for improving resources or creating new accommodation to support curriculum developments or boarding facilities can rarely be funded merely from fees.

The traditional method of fundraising for many schools has been the direct 'Appeal' for a particular project, such as an indoor swimming pool or new technology centre. Heads often draw on professional fundraisers to manage these appeals, who unfortunately may absorb high percentages of the money raised, thereby undermining the confidence of staff and parents, however impressive the appeal brochure. Increasingly, therefore, schools are adopting the initiatives of a longer term development programme run by a Development Director or Manager.

The characteristics of 'development' fundraising can be readily identified. Rather than launching one-off appeals every five or ten years, many schools are now recognising the greater value of continuous philanthropic support, especially if offered tax-efficiently over a number of years. Smaller **regular donations** by automatic bank debits soon mount up to provide sizeable gifts to the school, with relatively little financial impact on the donor. A well-targeted **legacy programme**, aimed at the appropriate alumni/ae age ranges, can reap significant dividends, even if sometimes these may not be accessible until well into the future.

The increasingly common practice of presenting an **Annual Fund** brochure to school alumni/ae and current parents can prove very effective. Specific items are identified, some of which may appeal to former pupils and others which attract gifts from parents whose children can benefit from the new resources over the following year. One development consultant has described this annual giving as 'the engine of development and the incubator of larger gifts to come'.

In addition, generating major gifts, particularly for capital projects, often requires careful and discreet research about potential donors among former pupils and current parents. The Freedom of Information Act provides access to valuable data on company executives and wealthy or 'high net-worth' individuals who may be associated with the school and, if handled appropriately, face to face 'solicitations' can reap generous rewards. The Head usually has a significant role to play in such encounters, particularly if these take the form of a dinner at the Head's private residence.

Friendraising

However, all such development initiatives for fundraising depend on two critical issues: first, an accurate and up-to-date parental and alumni/ae database and, secondly, an assumption that those approached to give will have a warm predisposition towards their school.

On the first issue, historically, alumni/ae records could well have been stored in someone's garage for decades, and may reflect periods of neglect when they were not maintained at all (perhaps when the school went through a 'rocky' patch). They may, as a result, have seldom been systematically updated. One of the major tasks of a Development Director is therefore to ensure that the data of former pupils are comprehensively and accurately recorded. The relationship between the development office and the alumni/ae association should ideally be characterised by partnership and cooperation, if progress is to be made. Personality tensions or over-defensiveness about 'boundaries' will create serious obstacles to effective fundraising.

A second critical issue is how alumni/ae feel about their old school. Was it a place where they were regularly bullied or beaten? Do they feel embarrassed because they have not lived up to the school's expectations of their career or resentful because they were constantly 'put down' at school? The Development Director needs to be highly sensitive to the gamut of emotions likely to be aroused in response to contact from the old school. Donations are unpredictable: one with a negative experience might want to give generously to improve the lot of current pupils, whereas another with a positive memory might feel the school does not really need his money.

The foundations of successful fundraising often depend therefore on the relationship with the school. In 'development' jargon this is called 'friendraising', and schools have adopted a variety of strategies to create the right climate for nurturing a giving culture. Alongside the accurate database already highlighted, interactive alumni/ae websites can be particularly effective at generating interest, as has been shown by the success of *Friends Reunited*: there is that natural curiosity to find out what happened in later life to Bloggs Minor or that apparently 'perfect' Head Girl.

Some schools have instigated telephone campaigns, where current senior pupils are trained to call former pupils, to ask them about their memories of school and to update them on exciting new developments since their day, thereby encouraging them to help fund new facilities. Utilising professional companies to organise this can be very expensive, but some Heads have considered the investment worthwhile.

If there are good relations between a development office and the alumni/ae association, there is great potential for hosting special occasions for particular generations of pupils: dinners, concerts, sports events all attract interest and renew friendships, providing opportunities for encouraging generous donations to their old school. If these events are hosted at the school, former pupils are usually delighted to see that familiar buildings are still in place, but now populated with the next generation of confident and welcoming young people.

How does the Head manage the oversight of development issues? What is the reaction of the staff? How does a development office influence the parents or the alumni/ae association? What impact does development have on a governing body?

An effective development programme depends on cultivating relationships, and the Head's role is critical to its success. Most Heads already expect to attend alumni/ae functions, and to enthuse about exciting new initiatives and recent pupil achievements. This may involve travelling abroad to 'network' with former pupils in the USA, Far East or Australasia – usually an enjoyable experience, although sometimes difficult to schedule around the pressures of running a school.

However, the establishment of a 'Development Office' in a school (assuming that space and additional personnel can be found) may prove very controversial. Staff are likely to resent its set-up cost, diverting valuable resources away from the classroom and into an area which, initially at least, will absorb far more money than it generates. If teachers are already rather sceptical about spending valuable resources on marketing, convincing them about the benefits of funding the creation of a development office in the school is going to be an uphill task.

Effective development directors will be sensitive to these issues. They must not push too hard to ingratiate themselves into the staff common room, however anxious they are about establishing their position and status in the school. Much will depend on the individual's personality, but a good development professional will endeavour to gain staff confidence through well-presented newsletters, involvement in staff social events and, perhaps most effective of all, encouraging staff to attend alumni/ae events, where they can enjoy meeting former students whom they have taught and perhaps lost contact with. In most cases, alumni/ae appreciate the chance to see their former teachers if only to convince them that they 'came good' in the end.

The Annual Fund process is also an important way of encouraging staff involvement in the development process. By identifying projects or resources needed by departments or boarding houses, colleagues can begin to see the benefits of fundraising to their own work, and that of the pupils. New resources funded by such donations are particularly appreciated if they allow the purchase of those 'high-tech' teaching aids which normal departmental budgets cannot afford.

The relationship with the Old Boys/Girls Association is also critical. Such associations can be rather fixed in their ways, and slow to adapt to new thinking – their prime purpose being to network and socialise through sports or other events. Encouraging them to be supportive and, hopefully, involved in fundraising initiatives requires tact, patience and persistence on the part of the Head and the development director. If a development office in the school can be established alongside the alumni/ae administration, there is real scope for mutual cooperation and greater efficiency, to the benefit of all parties.

How does the development director relate to the governing body? The Chair of governors is likely to be involved in his/her original appointment, and the creation of a Foundation or Development Board should provide governor oversight and representation: this board will also appoint distinguished alumni/ae as members, who may be interested in being potential governors. Regular reports to governors are essential, particularly as governors need to be encouraged, where possible, to lead from the front in giving if they are to convince others to be generous.

The Chair often writes the foreword to the fundraising brochures and ensures s/he endorses the work of the Foundation on public occasions. The governors also need to be confident that the significant expenditure on 'development' is well invested and donations properly managed, so that they can justify these to questioning parents. Accountability and transparency are paramount.

The relationship with parents must also be thought through carefully. Often the Parents' Association plays a major role in fundraising for additional resources for the benefit of their children's education – a role not dissimilar to that of the development office. Ensuring that activities and events complement rather than clash, supplement rather than compete, is an on-going priority. If relations are good, this cooperation can be highly beneficial.

To what extent should development directors be involved in school management? The development professionals or consultants usually recommend that directors should be members of the senior management team. This may be appropriate if s/he is directly involved in marketing and public relations for the school, but seems unrealistic otherwise. Presenting updates to senior staff on progress with fundraising should be encouraged, and may also be shared with all staff at general meetings, but development directors have little contribution to make to discussions, for example, about academic staffing or pupil progress tracking. Perhaps half-termly development reports to SMT, together with weekly or fortnightly meetings with the Head to monitor progress and facilitate communication, are an ideal combination.

Successful 'development' requires investment, professionalism, confidence and commitment. Nurturing potential donors is usually a long-term process, demanding patience and tact, but schools' expectations are too often for instant returns on the investment costs of setting up a Development Office. The Head's role is critical in ensuring that expectations are realistic, that development priorities are wholly in line with overall school development plans and that development directors are fully accountable, relating appropriately to all the varied constituencies which together make up a thriving school community. Development is more than just raising money: successful fundraising happens only when you have everything else right.

Chapter 11

Governors

Nigel Richardson

Remember two things. First, they don't have to do it, and we owe it to them to smooth their paths as much as we can. Most of the time, most of them will support and complement us with their expertise. Sometimes they will wisely caution us, drawing on their knowledge of a school over a much longer period than we have. Periodically they will surprise us, either with their knowledge or their lack of it. Sometimes they will inspire us with their strategic vision.

But there will also be some times when some of them will seem meddlesome, infuriating, even petulant. Even the best governing bodies can sometimes decide a big issue in two minutes, only to make heavy weather for three-quarters of an hour of something very trivial indeed. But ultimately it is a job that they don't have to do.

Secondly, we need them. We rely on their ability as non-executive directors – more or less – to stand back and view things strategically or with a detachment which we, who are too close to a situation, do not always have. We need to draw on financial, legal, marketing and planning skills (amongst others) which we may not always have either.

In an age when the responsibilities on trustees of charities grow all the time, we also need the legal protection which their presence affords us – and at times the knowledge that they are taking responsibility for financial decisions which may have an impact way beyond our own departure from the school.

Occasionally we need to hide behind them, when having to go for a difficult or unpopular set of decisions. And, if we are honest, it is probably good for those of us who spend all day giving orders to other people, occasionally to have to take them to higher authority. It's not easy though … and we should avoid the temptation to see them as the enemy within – even when the going is tough.

It is sometimes said that a good marriage is one which is worked on, and in which the two partners don't take each other for granted. Our relationship with our governors is much the same – or perhaps more like a series of simultaneous marriages (I hesitate to push the analogy too far). The fact that governors may sometimes *seem* insufficiently appreciative of our efforts and skills does not mean that they are – or that we should fail to appreciate them.

First and foremost, cultivate your relationship with the Chairman: absolutely crucial. Whilst you may not see eye to eye on everything, a united front in public and at board meetings should be preserved if at all possible. No man can serve two masters: the Chairman is in charge, and must be – both where the Head and the board itself is concerned.

Your relationships with each individual governor are important. These are many facets to this, because governors come in all shapes, sizes and personalities. Be wary of the constant questioner, and the one who rings you up every time he sees a hanging-out shirt within five miles of the school. Beware of the rhetorician: the governor who can swing a meeting with a few over-the-top strap-lines.

Learn to spot those who may be prone to lobbying by pressure groups of parents: too many dinner parties can be a dangerous thing, and one or two governors should get out less... But also resist the temptation – if you are given the opportunity to exercise it – to surround yourself with too many submissive cyphers and kindred spirits as governors: there is value in creative tension. It is said of some of the greatest long-serving Heads that in their final years they had their governing bodies completely sewn up, packed as they were with the Legend's friends and think-a-likes – and that, as a result, the school lost its strategic cutting edge.

On the other hand, you don't want to create *too* much conflict: the board's collective chemistry matters. In business a board's members are united by a clearly and fairly narrowly defined common purpose: schools should operate along much the same lines, with board members uniting in their goodwill for the school and a desire to do it good. In both situations, they bring varied individual skills and expertise to the table.

Succession planning – for future governors of all types – is important and too often overlooked. All boards should have search committees to identify new, additional skills-sets to the ones which they currently have. Most will have an attendance register, with mechanisms to remind frequent absentees that they are not pulling their weight. Wise boards will have a retiring age (probably 70); this can be broken in special cases, but it should happen only via an agreed mechanism which applies to all governors.

However, boards should also recognise the increasing value of those in their 60s who have time to contribute. An increasing number will put arrangements in place for external monitoring of the effectiveness of the board as a whole, although they may not yet have gone down the road of their USA counterparts in having a standing committee of trustees (with its own chairman), charged with the specific responsibility for scrutinising the effectiveness of both the board and its individual members. Above all, identify the *next* Chairman in good time.

Don't let governors steamroller you – even though they will be used to getting their way in their own spheres of life. Don't be afraid to be a little Machiavellian: you need to work out what *not* to tell them as well as what they should be told. There are some issues on which a new Head keeps them in the dark at his peril (some of them seemingly trivial): proposed changes to the uniform are probably one of these. You also need to guard against a situation in which something goes wrong and governors can say: "We never knew". That type of situation can be a hard one for a Head to retrieve.

The businessmen amongst them may need to be initiated in the subtleties and paradoxes of a sector in which schools and Heads are both friends and rivals, and in which one needs also to think of the overall educational provision in the area as a whole, as well as the interests of the school itself.

The businessman governor may well want you to seize every pupil you can, and drive the opposition to the wall by aggressive marketing.

But it won't win many long-term friends amongst feeder school Heads, and if a school closes in your area, and if you are unable to offer extra places in your school *next term*, there are a great many losers and losses – including, potentially, your reputation.

Your relationship with the bursar is just as vitally important. Should the bursar also be clerk to the board? There are pros and cons to this, dependent mostly on how well you get on with him (or her). I have worked both systems: if your bursar is a gem, there is no substitute to having your study and his office in close physical proximity – nor in the bursar having this dual role.

It cuts down time for both of you, by removing the need for an additional party to service the board whom you will both have to brief regularly (and, sometimes, it obviates the cost of paying someone to be the clerk). It also helps to prevent another possible source of division: bursar and clerk versus Head: Chairman and clerk versus Head and bursar *etc*. Provided that you and your bursar/clerk work together well, it makes for more harmonious relationships within the board.

But, if the bursar shows too many signs of wanting greater independence, or starts to open up a direct line of communication to the Chairman or individual governors without reference to you, it may well be sensible to aim to have these roles split. You also need to guard against having communications with the Chairman of which the bursar (whether clerk or not) is unaware, because by doing so, you will have created the very division that you want to avoid the bursar creating against you.

In the end, whichever system you have to work with, it is a fact that normally only you and the bursar will be directly employed by the governors (unlike your deputies) – with all the reduced job security which that fact implies. You need to plan carefully a united front before each meeting.

Time was, when a new Head succeeding someone after a long reign found that the board had postponed or shelved all new strategic thinking until the newcomer's arrival. Fortunately, this is now a thing of the past – so encourage the Chairman at an early stage to give you his view on the school's current position and future prospects, as well as any priorities which he/she and the board have already identified. (Many of these may well have emerged during the selection and interview process.)

Some boards will treat Heads almost as an equal; others will keep him or her more at arm's length – so how much room the Head will have for manoeuvre will vary from school to school. But unless the board is exceptionally disunited or unresponsive, an incoming Head can aim to take steps which make governors more inclined to respect both the role and the individual fulfilling it. I write 'aim to' because much of what follows will need to be done gradually, and can only be fully achieved with the Chairman's agreement. Much of it may already be in place when you arrive – but if it isn't, and if you can instil it, it will, in the long run, help you in your work.

From the outset, give your governors the respect which their voluntary donation of their expertise and interest deserves, by being efficient and producing high-quality paperwork. Respond to their individual queries and concerns quickly; if any of them overdo it, seek the Chairman's help in reducing the number of requests.

Many will be directors of companies in which the balance of executive and non-executive directors is much nearer to 50-50 than in a school in which you and the bursar are the only two executives: governors may tend to forget that fact. Some boards risk being all chiefs and no Indians – and retired people are especially prone to forget just how many things the Head and bursar have to do immediately, once the governors themselves have departed after the meeting.

On the other hand, there are also times to bite your lip, and to avoid taking criticism personally. The legal and other requirements on governors and charity trustees these days make it almost inevitable that the school's management will take a different view from the more zealous members of the board when the health and safety manual or the risk register are up for annual review.

Make sure that governors' papers are clear, well-presented and sent out well in advance. Provide them with both paper and electronic copies (if that is what they want) at least a week ahead of each meeting: they may well have to fit their reading around many other commitments.

Consider a governors' intranet for weighty papers, such as those policies which need annual updates. Aim to keep things brief where you can (few busy governors will read a paper of much more than four sides of A4 unless it is a major strategic document, and most will prefer one or two). Use bullet points and appendices. Give clear conclusions and recommendations and, if necessary, an executive summary.

You should aim to present a termly report as part of your board papers, but try not to give too much repetition of what you have already told the sub-committees: your aim with the governors as a whole is merely to inform those governors *not* on the various sub-committees of key issues. The chairmen of those sub-committees will probably themselves be reporting to the board as a whole.

Avoid the minutiae of school life which appear in newsletters (which the governors should receive anyway). In most schools, the full board meets towards the end of a term, to round off and confirm the work which the sub-groups have already done. And – if you are fortunate – to do some blue-sky thinking, too. Strategy is, after all, one of the main drivers of a dynamic board.

What is the ideal structure of the sub-committees? Most governing bodies will have estates and audit committees for which most of the paperwork will come from the bursar; a finance and general purposes committee which will probably receive more from the bursar than the Head (including draft accounts and budgets); and an education committee serviced largely by you and your deputies. There may also be prep and pre-prep school committees (if you are responsible for such schools) into which you and the relevant Head will have most of the input.

There may also be marketing and development (fundraising) groups. Try to avoid letting *ad hoc* groups proliferate, however – and where you have to have them, aim to control their activity through tightly-drawn agendas and minutes/action points: it is these groups through which governors are most likely to stray off-message or get out of control. Fundraising development groups are a notorious example of this, because by their very nature their business can spill over into so many unforeseen directions.

One other group is a must-have (at least, in my view). At one time – in my own experience – the Head's salary got fixed more or less on the back of an envelope as an afterthought when the board members were vanishing out of the door at the end of the summer term meeting. Things have changed: there should be a proper remuneration committee (perhaps the Chairman, chairman of F & GP, the staff governor and two others) taking both a year-on-year and strategic view of the salary levels of you, your deputies and (where relevant) the Head of the prep and pre-prep.

The bursar's salary should be considered by this committee as part of the exercise, and (s)he may wish to include his/her most senior staff. Again, it is important that you and the bursar agree the recommendations to be submitted – or at least record the points on which you have agreed to differ. Reporting in detail to this committee via a written report each June or July will also be a valuable discipline for you in assessing the effectiveness of your SMT.

Assuming that you are given some say in the matter, who from the SMT should attend the various governors' meetings? Again, much will depend on the particular structure of your schools and the personalities involved. In most schools, the Head and bursar will be in attendance at all meetings of the full board; in some, the senior school deputies and the prep and pre-prep Heads may also be present for all or part of the meeting. Development and marketing directors are increasingly included, too.

But where the full board is concerned, even if all these people are present for those parts of the meeting when the reports from the relevant sub-committees are being formally received or for discussion of long-term strategic issues, you should aim to have at least part of the meeting each term at which only you and the bursar are in attendance. The board's relationship with the two of you is a very particular one, given the terms of your employment. Furthermore, if this arrangement is *not* in place, you increase the chance of governors deciding to hold private business sessions (see later) from which you are excluded.

As a general rule, consider persuading the Chairman to have an SMT presence in varying proportions on all the various sub-committees. The first deputy and development director might well be on the F&GP, along with the junior school(s) Heads; any other SMT members might be spread across the rest. Deputies can gain experience of how governing bodies work this way – and we all have a responsibility to train them, either for headship or to take over from us in an emergency. The junior Heads should of course be on the sub-committees devoted to their constituent schools.

Should you aim to have other Heads on your board, and should you yourself be heavily involved in the governance of other schools? Some of the independent school associations recommend that at least one retired Head should be on the board – and that it should be someone selected by the Head for the Chairman to approve.

It can be invaluable to have a wise Head on the board as ally, critical friend, and an intermediary to explain to those governors (who once went to school themselves and who assume therefore that they know all about your job) that it is not always as straightforward as it might seem. There is much truth in the old saying. 'Appoint in haste: repent at leisure'. Choose carefully, and avoid those who collect roles, can't say no, are self-important or just unrealistic about the number of meetings to which they will be able to turn up.

Yes, the unrealists *do* exist – and there are a surprising number of this last category. So don't fall into the same trap yourself: a good and willing deputy with bright career prospects may be more use to another school as a governor than an already over-stretched Head – unless its situation is unusually problematic and requiring experienced hands.

And, if you do sit on another board, try not to make demands on the Head which you would not wish others to make on you. Savour the moment at which you tense up on hearing someone utter the words: "I think we should ask the Headmaster to produce a paper on this issue", only to remember that it is not *your* workload that is being added to.

In an age when the cost of large building projects has to be tightly controlled if costs are not to run away with you, it seems likely that an increasing number of schools will consider external management of a style provided by major project management companies. Run well, and with the project manager carefully chosen, this can be very beneficial in helping to contain the Head's (and bursar's) time and workload, but be prepared to keep the proliferating number of consultants called carefully to account.

Be prepared, too, to be open-minded about, and to embrace, all the latest market research and demographic prediction techniques that they bring with them. Coordination and management of the many aspects of a major project are vital. A mechanism appropriate to both the scale of the project and your school's management structure is essential.

I predict that this is a key area for future professional development of Heads. If your school goes down this road, be even more sure than usual, too, to keep in close touch with your Chairman: the number of monthly meetings which large-scale project management requires will almost certainly alter the dynamics of your governing body and your relationship with it.

Beware that the governors on the project steering group don't become too dominant, and thus a board within a board, by ensuring that all governors receive regular progress updates. You yourself may also feel, in such circumstances, that you are working for two boards at once. Do not forget your own management team and staff, either – their dynamics too can be affected. This (yet again) is where you and the bursar will need to work closely together.

Finally, what if (for whatever reason) the going gets rough, for you, as a Head? There is far too little literature about this, and much of what is available ducks the key questions. Fortunately, thanks to regular school inspection over the past 15 years, there are fewer big surprises, and the Head has objective evidence about the school's performance with which to confront unreasonable critics.

But there will always be some situations in which, either through their own fault or merely through circumstance, or because of a failure of collective chemistry, Heads find things starting to unravel. Experience shows that there are some predictable danger scenarios which precipitate this, too:

- boards which become split along generation lines – especially where former pupils constitute a high proportion of the governors;
- where the Chairman appoints a new Head and then steps down too soon after (s)he arrives;
- where the Chairman and the chairman of F & GP do not get on: the least successful board with which I've been associated was the one where the Chairman did not attend the F & GP committee, and its chairman became *de facto* an alternative authority. The Head never knew where he stood, and the board eventually split down the middle;
- where governors listen too much to pressure groups of parents;
- where there are too many governors who are also current parents;
- where there is a governor nominated by the staff who listens to their concerns too uncritically;
- where numbers or league table placings dip;
- where governors retreat increasingly into private business, with the Head (and sometimes the bursar) asked to withdraw. This is a very unsettling and largely pernicious practice except, perhaps, when the board is about to choose your successor – a process in which you should *not* seek to become involved!

It is impossible to give hard and fast rules in such situations except to urge you to flag up the warning signs early. The Associations are always keen that any Head sensing trouble ahead should immediately consult his/her elected or paid officer(s). They will be used to providing support, and will be willing to meet both the Head and Chairman if this might be helpful. If an agreed way forward seems unlikely, they may suggest that you enlist an ASCL field officer to negotiate severance terms and (occasionally, in extreme cases) to provide legal support against a board.

At such times, we all need detached and objective advice – and there are more people perceived to be members of the Great and Good who have been through this sort of thing than you might realise, as well as an increasing number of Heads (myself included) who would qualify to become founder members of the 'second-chance club'.

When all is said and done, and for most of the time, however, our job is wonderfully varied and unpredictable. And, if our governors can sometimes be like that too, try (as we return to where I started) to think positively about them. Use their expertise to the full. We need them – and they don't have to do it.

Chapter 12

Marketing

Martin Stephen

A cynic defined marketing as presenting only the truths you want to be known to the customer who does not realise that he or she wants your services. Independent schools have been superb at marketing themselves for centuries – almost as good as they have been at denying they have ever been involved in anything so vulgar.

Though he would have shrunk in to a lengthy sermon at the merest thought, Thomas Arnold's muscular Christianity and sterile curriculum was a best seller for a market who sent their sons to public school in order to prove that they would never need to earn a living, and who were basking in the illusion that there was a moral and religious element to gaining and holding an empire, as well as a commercial one. From that sterile curriculum we have moved to the independent schools cornering the market in students taking up the traditional sciences, maths and modern languages: superb marketing in an age where these crucial disciplines are an endangered species.

At the risk of over-simplification, independent schools fall into three categories where marketing is concerned. First, there are the schools that are so big, successful or arrogant as to think that they do not need it. Secondly, there are those, usually in a highly competitive marketplace, who buy in professional marketing services. Thirdly, and probably the largest category, there are schools who try to do their own marketing without paying exorbitant consultancy fees. I am not trying in this chapter to beat the professionals, but rather just to offer some pointers as to what has and has not worked in marketing schools over the past 20 years or so.

How important is market research? Bad schools operate a fusion principle, and often blow apart. Good schools operate on fission, and focus inwardly to generate vast energy. One side effect of the latter is that schools are often surprisingly ill-informed about how they are actually seen by the outside world. We are fooled into thinking we know how our school is perceived, because many of the parents we see are coming to confirm an image of the school that they have already picked up. Those put off by its image in the outside world simply never bother to come.

There are a number of simple and inexpensive ways to research the image and standing of the school. A number of parents nowadays will ask local shop-keepers and taxi-drivers, or (heaven help us) the bus drivers who bring the pupils to and from school what they think about it and its pupils. There is no reason why the Head, if it can be done incognito, should not do the same thing. Asking a member of staff to do it and report back is usually better: if the outcome is critical, Common Room members will take it better from one of their own, instead of thinking Machiavelli is alive and well in the Head's study, and simply using invented bad news to get them to do more work.

Feeder schools are crucial. Their Heads have two great powers. First, they know what parents think about your school. Secondly, what they say about your school will greatly influence what parents think about it. It's immensely time-consuming, but a private lunch or dinner with the top ten feeder school Heads, on a one-by-one basis, is the best market research available, and cheaper than hiring a consultant. The same is true for lunch or dinner with the editor of the local paper and/or its education correspondent, and with the education editor of a national paper for schools who recruit outside their locality.

A crucial piece of research should be the very brief questionnaire you give to each set of parents after they have had a tour round the school. Any more than one side of A4 and they won't fill it in. You need to squeeze in questions that drag out of the parents as briefly as possible a few crucial facts:

- What were they expecting to find when they came round?
- Were they surprised when they did so, and by what?
- The best thing about their tour?
- The worst thing about their tour?

- Did anything impress them?
- Did anything do the opposite?
- How were they treated by admissions staff?
- How could the school change the system to make it work better for them and their child?

It is absolutely crucial that this questionnaire is totally confidential, and that parents only append their name and address if they wish to. It is also essential that it comes with a pre-paid reply envelope.

Advertising: is it worth it? The most common mistake we make is to assume (not unreasonably) that the purpose of an advertisement is to attract people to visit, or to take up at a place at your school. In fact, very few parents, if any, make their choice on the basis of an advertisement. They do so on the basis of playground chatter, the standing of the school locally and nationally, the comments by other parents, and even on league table placings. The crucial role of advertising is that each advertisement imposes an image of the school on the public. Advertising lets you tell the public what type of school you think you are. This is why your advertising is a complete waste of space and money unless it goes hand in hand with decent market research.

A good advertisement is based on a marriage between how you are perceived externally and how you wish to be perceived. If St Custard's has been top of the league table placings since before the Reformation, it can take its academic status for granted, and might be better advised to show smiley faces and use the word 'happiness' at least twice, in order to offset its inevitable image as an academic sweatshop whose number of A grades at A level are only equalled by its numbers of suicides.

If King Canute's does not hold up particularly well under the league table scrutiny, it is better advised to base its whole advertisement round a pupil who got a place at Bristol to read medicine or whatever. After all, the strength of most of our schools is that they gain pupils the best results of which they are capable.

At all costs avoid trying to fiddle the best you can out of the statistics: 'Pupils at Queen Delirium's achieved 72.07% pass rate at grades A-C in their recent GCSE examinations, exceeding the national average by

12.85%. Delilah Clutterbuck and Sam Fountain Lickspittle achieved some of the highest marks in the country for wired sugar flowering…' *At all costs*, stop your advertising being smug, complacent and pompous, and stop it from looking hopelessly cluttered.

And have you considered what you are saying about your school in your job advertisements? There was a time when the inverse law of school crests held sway: the larger the crest in the *TES*, the lower the status of the school: correspondingly some of the most famous schools had apologetic little advertisements so small as to bring tears to the eyes of the advertising department.

How can you liven up your advertisements? Much of your time and money are wasted if your advertisement does not stand out. It grieves me to say it, but the professionals here can be worth what they charge. Interesting examples include the school whose sole advertisement was '39 ÷ ? = 13. If you're already working out what ? stands for, you might want to work on a place at …'. Then there was the advertisement for a Latin teacher written entirely in Latin, or the shameless bowing to modern youth culture and *Little Britain* with 'Computer says …YES! We have the best ICT suite in the country …'

Niche Marketing: at any given time there will be a number of schools who have latched on to an idea that corners, for them, a sector of the market. In the 1970s it was boys' schools taking girls into the sixth form. In the 80s it started to move to boys' schools going fully coeducational. Taking the International Baccalaureate has worked well for schools since the Millennium.

Interestingly, some schools do well by niche marketing single-sex education. One or two have always claimed to specialise in, for example, sending pupils on to read medicine or law. Does your school have or do something well that no, or only a few, other schools do in your region? The only word of warning is to be careful before cornering a niche that it does not become a backwater.

On a lesser level some schools have suffered by majoring on a given sport or activity as a marketing exercise. This can backfire in two ways. First, you court the danger of parents saying: "If he/she doesn't play rugby/hockey/rowing/three-day eventing/the violin there's no point in sending him/her there". Secondly, you lose out rapidly in the public perception if, in order to keep up your results, you have to offer so many sports or music scholarships that pupils who have been in the school for three, five or more years never get in to the senior first teams or orchestra.

There are three rules that really matter for marketing to prospective parents. The first is that the parents must have the chance to meet the Head. It's entirely reasonable for parents to want to see the person who will decide the direction of their child's school, whose management skills will do more than anyone else's to decide if the school works or not. How the meeting takes place can vary. The point is that it has to take place.

The second rule is that prospective parents must meet pupils. The most conventional way is to have whole or part of a tour done by pupils. The best thing about teaching and schools is the pupils, and it's very rare for a boy or a girl to let you or the school down. Yet you need to be cautious. The delightful young man or woman who becomes completely tongue-tied, or the mathematical genius who last actually spoke in a lesson three years ago, are not going to give your prospective parents what they need. If at all possible, brief your pupils without trying to restrict them or speak from a party line, and send them round in pairs: it makes a tour infinitely easier for all parties.

There's a simple trick that is invaluable, and increasingly common. Persuade a friend, or pay someone you trust (or preferably three sets of parents), to pose as a prospective parent, ring up the school, arrange a tour and visit. Let them come incognito, but tell your admissions staff that an unspecified number of ringers will be doing the business and reporting back on it. Let yourself be interviewed, and the ringers be taken round by a pupil or pupils.

Then ask them to report back fully on their experience, warts and all. Did you know that while they were waiting in the assigned area one of the school porters carefully made himself a cup of coffee, and drank it with relish in front of gasping parents who had been held up for two hours in a motorway gridlock? Or did you know that some wag had borrowed words from Philip Larkin and inscribed on the inside of the visitors' lavatory door: 'They f**k you up, schools. They don't mean to, but they do …'.

Even simpler: take an hour off one morning at the start of morning break, and drive in to school just as if you were a parent visiting it for the first time. Walk the tour, and try to look at it with fresh, parental eyes. Are there weeds in the flower beds? Is the paint really peeling off the entrance door where it has apparently been kicked by every pupil who passes through it? Is it really a layer of dust that thick on the artificial flowers that droop plastically in the hallway?

The third rule is not to shepherd prospective parents round a pre-ordained and inexorable route, rather like the first path cleared through the D-Day minefields. Let them and their prince or princess go where they wish – within reason – and make it a personalised tour even if you can't make it a personal one. Be prepared to be asked to see the school lavatories, which are often a vision of the real school – but no: don't let Dad go in to the ladies or Mum in to the gents.

Do be prepared to be asked why a parent should send their child to you rather than to someone else. Resist the attempt to slag off your competitors: parents hate it. You're marketing the school with every word you, your staff or your pupils speak, and you're not doing it well unless you know your school's USPs (unique selling points: what you do well, and preferably what you do best of anyone).

Most of all, don't claim perfection. Humans don't come perfect, and nor do schoolchildren; parents know that better than most. Many of the parents want to know what you and the school will do when the going gets rough. Will you cope with the troublesome teenager, will you keep the faith, and will you care?

How should you treat prospective pupils? When I showed my first set of parents round as a newly-appointed Head I was so proud of myself until, at the end, the seven year-old burst in to inconsolable tears and was led down the drive leaving puddles behind him. I was distraught, and because I knew the parents slightly (it was a small town), I rang them up. "Oh," they said, "it's a simple explanation why he was so upset. You didn't show him the loos." For this particular young man, if you didn't see it, it wasn't there. The result was the terrifying prospect of coming to big boys' school and presumably having to wrap your legs round your neck from 11am onwards. Only the best of us market as well to the child as we do to the parents. On that tour, or in the study, is an astute awareness operating on a totally different wavelength. There is no easy way round this, but forced jollity is not the answer. A few thoughts:

- Has someone asked the boy or girl what they are interested in before they come, so the tour can be personalised?
- Does your tour tactfully deal with the issues that a child might be considering? What's the food like? Are there communal showers and will I have to undress before other pupils?
- This place is so big! Where do I actually come to first thing in the morning; what is *my* space in this monster of a building?
- Simple marketing consists of having something a young child can read in your study for the inevitable moments when the conversation goes adult-stratospheric; putting chocolate biscuits out and having decent orange juice available in quantities unlikely to make the child sick; allowing a nervous child to spend a trial day in school.
- Feeder schools are the most vital marketing target, and the most difficult. After all, they market themselves and know all the tricks of the trade, and when those tricks are being played. More alarmingly, their ex-pupils and their parents gossip and report back like nobody's business, and at times in the Christmas term a decent prep or primary school Head will know more about the morale (and possibly even the morals) of your school than you do.
- Be very careful about mounting a feeder schools' sports/music/drama/activities day or weekend, unless you already run one successfully. I once counted ten such invitations on a prep school Head's desk. You are in danger of giving a lovely day out at your own expense to boys and girls who have already chosen to go elsewhere.
- The best marketing with feeder schools is a personal relationship with the Head. You help the Head do his own marketing if you enable him to tell parents that he knows you well, and has your direct line.

- Ring up the feeder school Head with scholarship and entrance exam results, preferably on the afternoon before the parents receive the letter. It flatters him, lets him prepare for both the good and the bad news, and lets *you know* if you've got something terribly wrong.
- *Always* do the obvious and get your pupils to write to their previous Head at half term in their first term.
- Invite class teachers, with the feeder school's knowledge and permission, to sit in lessons for half a day or day.

Schools are increasingly using bursaries as a marketing tool, and one by which they can project an image of the school as being meritocratic and socially acceptable. Fair enough, but watch out for the shot-in-the-foot potential. Nasty backfires can include:-

- 'Why should I pay a part of my fees to educate someone else's child as well as my own?'
- 'It's not fair: it's easier to get in if you're a bursary candidate than if you pay full fees!'
- 'I know it's politically incorrect to say so, but I don't want my child mixing with children whose only experience has been of schools where disruptive behaviour is the norm.'

Some other issues: beware using the dreaded league tables as a marketing tool. Once upon a time a certain school did very well indeed in the league tables. The Head had copies of the relevant pages from every national paper expensively framed, where they graced the walls of the main entrance. Next year the school plummeted, leaving dark marks on the walls where the articles used to hang. In marketing terms, those who live by the sword die by it.

Should you use a professional marketing consultant? The best of them tell you what you need to hear, and perhaps tell you things you would rather *not* hear. The worst of them tell you nothing you don't know, and don't do anything you or a bright member of staff couldn't do. Two things to watch out for: first, a marketing consultant who works for lots of schools can find it hard not to impose a house style, with the result that your marketing takes on an *if-it's-Friday-it-must-Florence look.*

Secondly, and rather bizarrely, some marketing professionals still think it's all about brand familiarity. For an isolated rural boarding school, that can be true. For many other schools, it's not. It's about brand identification. Many independent schools have been around forever, and are household words either nationally or in the locality they serve. They don't need the community to be made aware of their existence; they need to be made aware of the special and unique features that turn the school from a household word in to a living and breathing entity.

The best thing that a marketing consultant can do is give you a marketing audit: check how you are perceived in your customer area, see if you could reasonably expand in to any new market and run a quality check on your in-house marketing.

The sad and rather frightening truth? Marketing can paper over the cracks in the initial stages of parental and pupil choice. But when the parents visit you and see the truth – which is actually what marketing is all about – marketing that is demonstrably a lie will do you infinitely more harm than no marketing at all. Hell hath no fury like a parent marketed in to believing a lie.

Chapter 13

Public Relations

Tony Little

The panel of national newspaper correspondents was bemused: question after question from the gathering of Heads asked them why newspapers did not write more stories, better stories, nicer stories about the good things happening in their schools. The journalists clearly thought that they did: the Heads clearly that they did not. One thing was indeed clear – that there was little understanding between the two groups.

Most Heads will say that the way their school is portrayed in the media, or not portrayed, is their greatest public relations concern. Yet in some ways this is a strange reaction. Having been Head of one school where it felt as if a tornado ripping its way through the school grounds would merit the merest ripple in the national press, and another where the breath of a comment is the stuff of headlines, the question arises what difference press interest has actually made. Both are very good schools, thriving, confident in their identity and purpose. Both are well regarded and recruit well. A fashionable name in newsprint appears not to make much difference.

This experience highlights a golden rule of public relations: it is the way a school communicates with its own community that matters most. The rest follows. Repeated surveys over a number of years show that prospective parents are most attracted to a school by personal recommendation, an endorsement from current parents or meeting a pupil who impresses them. Word of mouth is the most potent weapon, and potential problem, for our schools. Dinner party chat and car park gossip can be way off the mark and create an issue where there had been none, but in the main the members of our communities – parents, current and former pupils, and staff – want to be believers and spread the word.

Good communication is therefore the key. Yet most people in school communities will say that communication in their school is poor, or at least not good enough. It is one of the axioms of school life. Schools are busy, complex places but communicating the level of information individual people might feel they need is a difficult, even impossible, task. I was once chided by a senior colleague in a large school for failing to inform Common Room about the expulsion of a particular boy. In this case, it turned out to be a well formed hoax devised by pupils – the boy did not exist. Even transmitting good news can be problematic, one person's public praise is another's irritating detail; yet omitting a small detail can provoke a disproportionately anguished response.

Difficult though the task of communicating with the community may be, it is necessary and important in two ways. In the first place, schools need to sustain and enhance relationships through regular, individual contact. At this personal level, housemasters (or their equivalent) are central figures. Parents respond well to receiving regular snippets of news about their child. A note, a phone call, an email about good things done, help create the human contexts which make the difficult times easier to deal with: with good contact established, difficult news can be communicated early and lightly.

Parents wish to know that their children are being looked after by people who really do take an interest and who care. End-of-term reports, time consuming though they are, form a lasting record of a relationship. The Eton tradition that the housemaster writes a personal letter to the parent each term, not a standardised report, is one way of respecting that relationship. In similar vein, letters written about house achievements can have more impact than lofty pronouncements about the school as a whole.

There are, however, ample opportunities to beat the drum for the school as an institution, from assemblies with pupils to speech days and the website. In this last particular, news or sports or house pages untouched for months convey a telling message, though probably not the one intended. One line of approach to school news would suggest that all and any item should be writ large, on the lines that all publicity is good.

Yet the impression conveyed can be confusing. What prominence or weight should stories be given? Without a clear view of what it is the school wishes to project about itself, this question is impossible to answer. Of particular value here is a coherent statement about the school's distinctiveness. This is not a mission statement of the standard 'we produce fully rounded individuals' type, but a focus on specific strengths and qualities – those features that should be highlighted strongly, clearly and regularly.

To be effective, such a statement is not the kind of thing a management team can knock up in an afternoon: it needs to evolve from wide consultation involving teachers, pupils and parents, past and present, and alumni. Ask them the question, 'Why is the world a better, or at least different, place because our school exists?' and be prepared to be challenged by the answer.

Notwithstanding the time-consuming nature of such communication and the pressure of other priorities, it is by these means that the broad school community is given the shared knowledge, belief and confidence to be powerful advocates and effective recruiting sergeants: public relations at its best.

It is in this context that relations with the media should be seen. A watering of publicity, consistently applied, nurtures the community's sense of itself. Playing with the media in the expectation that buoyant, sustainable recruitment will follow is an illusion – and may well backfire. As one head-magisterial colleague put it: "The people who choose my school on the back of a story in the newspapers are almost always the least supportive members of it".

Establishing sound relationships with the local media is an obvious, though sometimes neglected, starting point. They have many pages and minutes of airtime to fill, and they usually respond positively – even enthusiastically – to the offer of items, both of the hard news and 'fluffy' variety. As with all news outlets in the modern media circus, they are often under considerable pressure of time and they may be happy to have the work presented to them on a platter. The small town local paper may well take your copy and print it verbatim. Larger regional papers and the airwaves media are much less likely to do so, but will respond to an intelligently framed angle on a story – particularly if it is hung on a quirky human element or plays against expectation.

If a school has a distinctive image in the public mind, a story that appears to play against type is often attractive and may help shift some perceptions as well; ballet lessons in a noted rugby playing school, the conspicuously privileged dealing with the problems of the under-privileged, and so on. It is remarkable how powerful an allure this can be. The presence of a writer-in-residence at Eton (part of a well-established scheme) who happened to be black and to have written some poetry deemed by some to be 'punk' merited the lead arts story, over several pages, in the *New York Times*.

Some Heads are irritated by the idea that precious time be wasted 'courting' local journalists, but it is time well spent, not just to spread a comforting glow of achievement in the locality, but in order to have some good feeling in the bank to set against more trying times. Friendly, known faces from the local press and balanced, sensible reporting were a boon in the aftermath of a dreadful school minibus crash. By contrast, I well remember the look of dismay in the eyes of a national reporter when it became apparent that there would be no fatality, which disappointment prompted him to an excess of zeal in his coverage of peripheral issues.

Much though it may sound like some GCSE empathy role-play, it is worth trying to understand the journalists' perspective and the practical limitations within which they operate. However well-disposed journalists might be, their sub-editors will demand stories with a punch that will sell. Some while ago, I was rung by a young-sounding journalist from a distinguished national with a reputation for balance. She asked me about the school's drugs policy. To my surprise, she rang back about an hour later to check that she had accurately recorded what I had said. It turned out that she had been on the paper for three weeks. When the story appeared two days later, having been shaped, improved, and doubtless made 'more interesting' by the sub-editor, the balance had gone, one half of my observations were reported, and with a slant, and the piece was introduced by a racy headline.

More recently, I succumbed to the approaches of a senior journalist from a national Sunday paper who wished to write a piece about the school 'as it really is'. He seemed sensible and positive, and so he proved to be, spending time in lessons, with pupils and staff. At the end of his time, he spoke very warmly about the school.

In the event, his article reflected that warmth and had good things to say, but then there was a change of style and tone and a degree of chippiness and rather worn language; it was a worthwhile piece, but very much a mixed bag. Shortly after publication, I received a hand-written note from the journalist saying that it had been a pleasure, and so unusual, to write such a whole-heartedly positive piece about an institution. Clearly, that was as good as it gets. We felt somewhat under-whelmed and a little irritated.

The underlying point is that even with well disposed journalists from the national press a Head will be unlikely to read a piece that will give him unalloyed joy. It would be foolish to believe otherwise. If the thrust of an article or reference is broadly positive, that is an achievement. Always remember that for the journalists, their stories must be prompted by the *national* debate. The issue for an individual school is where it fits into that debate – which will seldom allow for a full account of the school's character. As it happened, the drugs piece was not wholly misleading and at least made it look as though the school was trying to do something about a difficult social issue; and the Sunday article was generally well received by people both inside and outside the school community. Heads can sometimes feel too deeply about inaccuracies and misrepresentations.

One can, of course, never really judge how a news story will be interpreted. Some 20 years ago, when the news broke that some of their peers had perpetrated a shocking sequence of burglaries in a nearby housing estate, boys in my boarding house rushed in to my study waving shaming, lurid headlines, "Sir, sir," they shouted, "it says we are a *top* public school".

There is seldom a way to avoid bad news of the sort that attracts vibrant media attention, be it of the errant scoutmaster variety or a disaster: schools exercise a powerful place in the minds and hearts of adults, and rightly so. As a Head, one has to be prepared for grim moments. And there is a way to be prepared. Crucially, the school community, certainly the staff, need to know that they must react swiftly in the event of a potential problem, and also know whom they should contact: the Head's secretary perhaps.

If there is time to prepare a press statement, have it written and in the top drawer of the desk. If not, respond quickly to media interest – it can significantly help shape the way the story is framed. It can be helpful to issue a holding statement on the lines of: 'There will be a press statement at 4pm and all questions will be answered then'. The timing is a matter of judgement and will depend on the seriousness of the incident.

Whichever route is chosen, be factually accurate, and make sure that the facts are secure – having to correct a version of events later is damaging. In the fast moving world of e-technology, the first news story usually sets the tone for the rest. Journalists often feed off each other. If the story is particularly big, the Head will need competent colleagues who know what to do (or a professional agency with whom a relationship has already been established) to share the burden.

As I have discovered, a Head alone can not hope to cope with 24 contacts from the national and international press in the space of a couple of hours. Unlikely though the need might appear, it really is worth planning for such an eventuality, especially by building a close group of trusted colleagues who can swing into action at a moment's notice.

Fear of adverse reaction, of becoming the coconut on the pole, can prompt some Heads to keep as far out of harm's way as possible. This is a natural reaction – we Heads did not intend a life in the glare of publicity, we are schoolteachers with an interest in young people. Yet it is a pity if Heads hide behind the parapet. We have a right, an obligation even, to speak out about matters of importance for young people and their education. And the time is ripe. Education is more of a public focus now than it has been. Rather than seeking only to promote the peculiarities of our own particular schools, we serve the cause of education *and* our schools better by commenting purposefully on the educational issues that concern us. What better impression in the public mind than to associate one's school with educational matters of substance and moment: standing up against bureaucracy and incompetence; standing up for the values that define our beliefs.

If such increased opportunity exists, it might be tempting to assume that a professional public relations officer would give weight and cutting edge to a school's profile. This is unlikely to be the case, not least because schools are not in a position to compete financially for people of quality in this area. I doubt whether such a person is necessary. It is the Head who embodies the culture of the school and who must be at the centre of its public relations.

What is needed are creativity and focus, best found, in my experience, by gathering together a group of lively people associated with the school who can critically review and spark ideas about all aspects of external relations, from signposting to television broadcasts. What is certainly not needed is the well intentioned parent or governor with some marketing or PR experience giving unsolicited advice from the outside – and such advice will surely follow in the vacuum created by an absence of organisation.

With the kaleidoscope of additional pressures on any Head, it is important to ensure that there is a structure designed to encourage a flow of ideas and to pre-empt difficulties. Such a structure benefits from a lack of rigidity and formality, but it needs the guarantee of proper time given over regularly to thinking things through, checking that the broad thrust of PR is reinforcing the distinctive elements of school life in a positive way. In short, in the tumble of daily activities, thinking of this kind needs to be given a priority.

Good organisation and creative thinking are needed in two areas of public relations that are particular considerations for our schools these days. First, fundraising has become a profession and an art form all of its own, but the basic principles obtain. In this case, however, a good professional makes a great deal of difference, as a reassurance and personal support to the Head, but principally as someone with the time properly to develop a team, build a sound structure and create and maintain a database that is accurate and helpful.

To the Head for whom this activity is new territory, two cautions: fundraising always takes longer than you think, and there will be plenty of rebuffs. Even in America where this is an established and core activity, a flourishing fundraising team with many years' experience will do very well to elicit positive responses from just half the school's alumni and parents. As with most things to do with PR, preparation reaps dividends. The adage that 'friendraising comes before fundraising' sounds trite, but holds true. What quicker way to lose a benefactor than to surround him with silence, to ask for money out of the blue and then, if given, to ignore him. The degree of sophistication evident in the operations of leading American institutions may not be relevant in our schools, but the underlying notion that success is built on developing and sustaining personal relationships is essential.

Secondly, at a time when our schools' connections with the broader community, and charitable status, are under scrutiny, the way we show the school's face to the world has become more important. Most independent schools have good stories to tell. Eton, for example, has run a residential summer school for state school young people for over 20 years, a commitment unsung and largely un-remarked.

In Oakham there would be no annual arts festival in the town, if it were not for the school. There are many examples of notable, beneficial activities of this kind undertaken by our schools because it has seemed the right thing to do. For some Heads it goes against the grain to promote educational and charitable matters which are our natural and proper activity, but we should be unabashed apologists for our school's cause.

In all aspects of our school's life, if we do not tell our story, others will either ignore it or tell it in a way that is misleading, unfair or plain wrong. This is not a case of 'spin', a short-term and short-lived response to the moment, but a story of integrity. In the end the school and its Head must be themselves, and that is the story to tell. People are deeply sceptical about efforts to woo or dazzle them; they want trust, not perfection. Good PR is about telling a true story as well as you can.

Chapter 14

Visible presence ... or bureaucrat behind the desk?

Vicky Tuck

The earlier chapters have established the wide range of the Head's leadership responsibilities and the various groups of people with whom you have a relationship or to whom you are accountable. Both the strategic and operational aspects of the Head's role are crucial and require skilful use of time.

The need to be accessible, visible and cheerful to pupils, staff, parents, prospective parents, alumni and governors – not to mention the local community – will almost certainly result in working very long hours and can sometimes give rise to a feeling that the workload is intolerable. In this chapter, while there is no pretence to provide all the answers, suggestions are offered for managing the workload and striking the balance needed for success in your role.

Guides to time management will advise you to prioritise and to distinguish between that which is urgent and that which is important. The difficulty in Headship is that you are both leader and servant of your school, of your staff, of your pupils and of your parents. Your strategic priority may be to redesign the tutoring system, review the school's catering or introduce an annual appraisal system, all of which will require a great deal of careful consultation – but it is essential to respect and make time for the priorities of others: the head of department who has received complaints about the teaching of one of his colleagues; the worried mother whose daughter is unsettled by her parents' divorce;

or working through the bursar's draft of the annual report by tomorrow morning.

And, even if you are adept at combining your own objectives with being accessible to others, sometimes, calmly, you will have to rearrange your schedule to make way for the unexpected such as a disciplinary incident where your authority, judgement and visible presence will be essential.

A Head is rightly expected to know his school well, to be able to assess how far it is meeting its declared aims and to assure quality. You can assess the quality of what is happening in your school in a variety of ways: gathering and, sitting at your desk, analysing data such as subject take up at GCSE; exam results by department; absence levels among staff; entry to selective universities or departmental expenditure.

However, much of your quality assurance will be achieved by going out and about to observe. Just as all guides to prospective parents encourage them to note attitudes of pupils and staff and the state of the facilities as they are toured around the school, so you must visit the four corners of your empire on a regular basis. Your appearance will be noted positively as you pick up litter, remove an out of date flyer from a notice board or turn off the lights in an empty room – although it will probably never be deemed to be frequent enough.

The suggestions which follow are recommended ways of 'walking the talk'; you could shadow a pupil or a member of staff for a day, to understand the school experience from their perspective; observe all new staff teach in their first year (and give them constructive feedback); go to the staffroom at break as often as you can; if yours is a boarding school, have lunch or supper with pupils in each house each term – with an arrangement with the housemistress to organise your visits so that over the course of the year you meet with every pupil; arrange a year group work scrutiny by the leadership team across all subjects; some weeks, where possible, go to someone else's office for your regular meetings rather than have them come to you; prior to your development plan discussions, divide up the entire school premises and allocate an area to each member of your team to scrutinise in terms of maintenance and aesthetic appeal. All these activities are worthwhile and enjoyable.

Your job is about 'being' as well as 'doing' and your diary for the term will include many occasions when you are simply 'there' – matches, plays, concerts, assembly, social functions for parents and so on. You should never underestimate how much your attendance is noted and appreciated – especially by those who have done all the hard work. Above all, though, these are opportunities to savour the quality of the education your school is providing and to be heartened by it.

Too often, a Head's day may have been full of difficulties: a tricky situation with a group of pupils; an underperforming member of staff; a disgruntled parent or news of a malfunctioning boiler! And you may have more underlying worries about pupil numbers or pressures on expenditure, so it is important for your own sanity and perspective to attend a spine-tingling concert and to be reminded that most people in your school are doing an excellent job and most pupils are a delight. So, as far as possible, avoid sacrificing due to workload your attendance at all these events that make your school a community rather than just a business.

Your most vital weapon in the war on workload is your personal assistant. She must be capable and committed to supporting you with absolute discretion. Spending time discussing and agreeing how she will manage your diary will prove very fruitful. Agree with her how much of your diary can be made available for arranging meetings, and how much time needs to be set aside for dealing with paperwork, or being out and about.

It is crucial to get the balance right if you are not to feel that you have lost autonomy. There will be days packed with consecutive meetings, and you can amaze yourself by your ability to manage this schedule, but meetings invariably involve some preparatory work or some follow-up and time must be allowed for this. As far as is possible, it is prudent to try to write the file note or the follow-up report or letter as soon as you can while your memory is still fresh.

On day-to-day matters, if she is good, your PA will allow you to maximise your time by exercising her judgement: she will know which calls you need to take and which are better passed to someone else. For those you must take, she will establish the subject matter for you, getting out any relevant file. For example, she will prepare your papers for meetings in such a way as to minimise your own preparatory work to those parts that only you can do. She will draft letters for you. When you are out of school, she will judge when to contact you and, for your return, she will have prioritised your mail.

The more you allow it, the more she will use her initiative and be pro-active. She is likely to be highly skilled in using technology, so rely on her to undertake research for you, set up spreadsheets, manage your diary electronically and use an information management system so that you are prompted, supported and have excellent records. As your relationship develops, talk to her about how she might help you more, and about how you work. She may have some valuable observations to make about your idiosyncrasies and some helpful tips.

If your first and most vital asset is your PA, your second is your ability to delegate effectively. When you take up your Headship, you will inherit a management structure and a team of people. They may all be excellent, and they will all need to adapt to working with you. Soon you will know whether you trust their abilities, and this trust is the prerequisite to effective delegation.

The other prerequisite is your own self-confidence to resist micro-management. Effective delegation means spending time at the outset agreeing expectations. Although it is vital to have many strengths as a Head – and it is certainly necessary to have a clear vision and to be prepared to take responsibility for the difficult decisions you may have to make – you can only succeed if you succeed through others and, provided they are aware of your exacting high standards, your team will enjoy their roles more if they feel trusted to show initiative and motivated by your support.

Some Heads will choose to have a series of regular meetings with each person they manage directly, in parallel with a meeting of the leadership team. Others have the latter, but meet with individuals only when and if they have a specific matter to discuss. Meetings serve a number of purposes: to monitor progress with agreed objectives and to discuss performance in areas of delegated responsibility; to support, motivate and advise; to keep the Head informed of issues associated with individual pupils, parents and staff; to prepare for public events.

Each Head must work out what suits his leadership style and the size of the school, but whatever approach you choose, you need to strive for maximum benefit from each meeting. This implies, once again, particularly in the case of meetings of a group of people, good preparation, documents circulated in advance, a clear idea of your desired outcomes and careful chairing to ensure that everyone feels able to contribute – but also that the agenda is covered in a time-efficient way. Above all, train yourself to pounce on volunteers, and to designate tasks to other members of your team, rather than commit yourself to undertaking a sizeable piece of work that has been deemed necessary!

Once you have completed a full year, it is worth looking at the pattern of the year and the differing demands made on you each month. Is the schedule realistic or could alterations be made that would allow you to be more effective? For many Heads the spring term is generally regarded to be the most crowded: entrance and scholarship examinations; recruitment of staff; development plans and budgets to be discussed and produced for consideration by the governing body. If much of this is immutable, perhaps there are other commitments which could be moved into the autumn or summer terms.

If you have ascended to the role of Head by taking on increasing responsibility in the teaching profession, you already possess significant organisational skills. Teachers' lives are characterised by preparing for and meeting deadlines: Year 9 first thing on a Monday morning; finishing the exam syllabus; report writing deadlines and so on. The Head will also have a series of deadlines to meet: a speech to give; a report to the governors to write; the leadership team meeting to chair.

Your well-honed high standards of professionalism are entirely transferable to planning ahead to allow sufficient time to prepare for these important commitments. Just as your pupils judged you on the quality of your lesson without appreciating the time involved in preparation, so you will be assessed by your staff, pupils and parents on how you perform on these occasions.

Just because you may have a bit more choice on what to do when, it is still essential to plan your unallocated time carefully, and not to procrastinate. At the same time, if you have perfectionist tendencies, you must conquer them. This may simply be a question of leaving yourself only just enough time to write that assembly or speech remembering that: 'The best is the enemy of the good'.

It is vital in the competitive world of independent education to see the big picture, to keep up-to-date and to encourage your leadership team to do likewise. However, the endeavour to remain well-informed can feel relentless and, since you will be bombarded with a staggering amount of unsolicited mail as well as receiving publications from your membership organisations, it is advisable to be decisive about your own priorities, so that you can select what to feed to your brain and what to consign to the wastepaper bin, virtual or otherwise, or rather to the recycling sack.

One approach is to decide what you need to be informed about for strategic purposes, and what you need to know about for operational purposes. For the latter you need to take note of, and act on, legislative and curriculum change in particular and, depending on your priorities, you may be interested in whatever is topical – personalised learning, virtual learning environments or how to fundraise, for example.

But for the former, the scope is much wider. We need to run our schools and prepare our pupils for the twenty-first century so it is important to set time aside for reading about socio-economic change, environmental challenge, the changing world of work, globalisation and so on. It is also desirable to be reasonably familiar with the views of the opinion formers in the education world, and to be up-to-date about higher education.

The internet is a very useful tool in this respect and the daily news digest which ISC will email to you has proved a most welcome short-cut to the most relevant articles on education. There is no magic formula for how to cope with the deluge of reading material, but a ruthless PA who is aware of your priorities and the roles of other staff will sift much away, and a gifted one will earmark important reading for you. It would be wrong to say 'ignore the lot', as you need to have an injection of opinion and ideas to help your restless questioning about the quality and evolution of your school's provision.

Technology provides a wonderful tool for managing your workload and communicating with your constituents. However, it can also be the bane of your life! Email renders you accessible to all your staff, all your pupils and all your parents in a way that was not the case in the past, when your PA acted as gatekeeper. Yet provided you are running your school well and delegated responsibilities are clear, you will not be bombarded by emails from pupils or parents.

Those who *do* contact you direct will usually have something valuable to say – so respect this by responding promptly. Email is also invaluable if, between one staff briefing and the next, or between one parents' mail out and the next, you want to tell them about something significant or urgent. An office management programme also facilitates recording, communication between meetings and gives you a tracking, filing and reminder system for each of those who reports to you.

However, managing the volume of emails in a large school can be daunting and, furthermore, the 24-hour access can find you working late into the night, simply in an attempt to deal with the inbox. Here too, the Head has to balance the desire to focus on achieving his own strategic objectives with being available to those who need to seek his guidance.

Email is dangerous in the way that it can dictate how a Head spends his time and it is advisable to decide to restrict the times at which you open your inbox to avoid distraction, especially when engaged on a task requiring undivided attention. Finally, schools should have an email code of conduct and the Head must set the standard in terms of decorum. If you have something difficult to say to a member of staff, it is much better to meet (and then record the meeting). Similarly, if a parent sends a heated email, avoid responding hastily, reflect and, probably, pick up the phone to diffuse the situation.

As you become more established, you will be approached to take on other roles, perhaps in the local community, for one of the membership organisations or on the governing body of another school. It is easy to be flattered to be asked and less easy for some to formulate that monosyllabic word: No – partly because you would not be in the role you are in if you were a clock-watcher, and the sense of service is very strong.

However, you may need to be more self-preserving and an affirmative to the following questions should exist before you take on more: Will taking this on be positive for my school? Do I have something to contribute? Will taking this on be positive in terms of my own professional development? If I do this can I give something else up? Will this put unnecessary strain on my personal relationships?

In conclusion, you need great emotional and physical stamina to be an effective Head, as well as skills as both a leader and an administrator. The days are long and intellectually demanding, and, especially if you are running a boarding school, will be accompanied by many evening and weekend commitments, but the holidays provide time to work to a different rhythm, to undertake planning and major research and to reflect and review (as well as to tidy your office).

This is a luxury that is not afforded to the CEO of other businesses, and should not be underestimated. But, unlike the CEO of other high quality service providers, notwithstanding your wherewithal to delegate, you are expected to be omniscient and omnipresent. You also need to be time efficient: everyone can appear busy but not everyone is busy on the right tasks and Heads need to be ruthlessly honest with themselves about how productive they are being.

That said, a day spent talking to a range of different people, motivating them and helping them to manage aspects of their workload but which ends without you having tackled some of the tasks on your own list may have been much more fruitful than you think. So, respect the needs of others and be flexible, not fretting if your schedule has to be abandoned or you feel you are drowning in paper, and learn to trust that you will meet all your deadlines. A tidy desk is a means to an end, not an end in itself and you do not want your obituary to read: 'He worked long hours but we never saw him'.

Finally, however overwhelmed you feel, make every effort you can not to complain to others. This can be difficult to do but bear in mind that you are likely to be the most highly paid person in your organisation and you are expecting all your staff to work hard. You have made a choice to take on the hugely demanding but hugely rewarding role of Head and you cannot expect to motivate staff if you are complaining about your workload. Neither can you expect praise as a Head but you will earn tacit respect for your own commitment as long as you do not whinge!

Chapter 15

Look after yourself

Marion Gibbs

People who know me may well be smiling wryly, if not actually laughing out loud, at the idea of my being asked to write a chapter on issues such as life-work balance. I was perhaps rather slow to learn the art of saying 'no', but after 13 years of Headship, I am now ensuring that I make more time for a personal and social life. This chapter is, however, about more than just maintaining a social life: I have been asked to reflect also on family life, personal space, quality of life, thinking time and areas of stress.

It would be foolish to pretend that becoming a Head does not have enormous implications for your personal life. However much you are determined to maintain a sensible life-work balance, it is very easy to become wedded to your school, and to focus on it to the exclusion of almost all else. Such an intense relationship is not healthy: it can lead to a loss of a sense of proportion, guilt at spending time on anything not connected with school, an inability to relax and enjoy anything outside school, overtiredness and stress.

Of course, we love our schools, feel excited by them and passionate about them, but we need to have a life of our own as well. This not only helps to make us more balanced Heads but it will also enable us to have a more enjoyable retirement. The caricature of a Head unable to cope with retirement, bereft of his or her school, and long since having lost touch with all outside friends and interests, has been a reality for one or two ex-Heads of my acquaintance.

Remember that CV you submitted when you applied for the post of Head – what interests and activities did you list there? Those who appointed you were doubtless attracted to the idea of your rounded, well-balanced character, and it is important to try to maintain this. It is a mistake to give everything up, all those friends, interests, passions, the family visits and holidays which helped to make you the person that you are and which will sustain and refresh you during and after Headship.

How much or how little you involve your family in the life of the school is a very personal choice – there is no single best model. Certainly if you are a Head of a boarding school, you will very probably be living on site and if you have school-age children you may choose to send them to the school. If you are Head of a more isolated country school, there may be no practical alternative to educating your children at the school, even if you or they would prefer otherwise.

Until quite recently, almost all wives of Headmasters in independent schools were expected to take on a support role, entertaining visitors, running committees and being a very visible presence: indeed, they were usually paid a salary to do this. Times have changed and many Heads' wives now have their own careers outside the school.

The situation for husbands of Headmistresses has always been different; married female Heads were almost unheard of until some 50 years ago (it was only in 1944 that it became illegal to sack a female teacher just for being married). Some Heads' husbands are very happy to support their wives at a myriad of school functions; others prefer to lead a life quite independent from the school. Such matters need to be discussed openly from the start and a suitable compromise reached.

Similar issues can arise for a single Head, as well as those in long-term partnerships. What if one is, or becomes, involved in a serious relationship: should one bring a partner to school events? Are all non-married school Heads expected to lead chaste lives? Discretion is definitely required, but not all school communities are the same. The secret is to know and understand your community and then to try to be true to yourself (although it is wise to make sure that you have the Chairman of governors on board first!).

Maintaining friendships with those who are completely unconnected with school is vital, whether you have a partner or not. You need to be able to relax and be completely at ease, something which may not always be easy, or even sensible, to achieve in the presence of current or past parents, staff and pupils. However busy you are, try to keep in contact with old friends, people who know you as you, not as the Head of a school. Certainly in areas such as London, schools and Heads are a mainstay of dinner party gossip.

On becoming re-acquainted with some people whom I had last met at university more than 30 years ago, I was amazed to discover how much I had since been discussed. They told me how they knew all about where I lived, through a distant connection with one of my neighbours, and reeled off names of their friends whose daughters were attending or had been pupils at the school, and even those whose daughters had *not* gained admission. One is rarely off duty as a Head: people notice what you are doing, where you are, what you are wearing, who you are with and how you behave. Accepting a third glass of wine, especially if you are female, can lead to rumours of alcoholism!

Some Heads choose, or may be obliged, to be at the heart of everything that happens in their local community, serving as president of all local societies, attending every local function, wining and dining with local families, including those of pupils. If this is your situation, it is important to establish a clear boundary between the professional and the personal or social.

My personal choice has been never to accept social invitations for meals or drinks with parents. First, I remember being told on my arrival how the whole sixth form timetable had just been re-written to accommodate one particular pupil's subject combination after my predecessor had dined with her parents. The timetable certainly had to be re-written to accommodate this pupil, although what prompted this cannot be known for certain. The fact that the staff believed it to be the result of a dinner party promise is significant enough.

Secondly, we have almost 800 pupils in the senior school: just under 1100 if one includes the juniors. I could not hope to dine with all their families, nor would I wish to show any favouritism, or to set up any competition to outshine one another in hospitality. That is my personal choice; other Heads choose differently. What is important is to make sure that how you feel about such things is well known and properly understood. Needless to say, I am vice-president of many local societies and attend lots of local functions, but that is not the same as socialising privately with school families. The boundaries for those with their own children are more complicated – but most Heads seem quickly to become adept at being 'Elizabeth's mum' one moment and the Head the next.

For much of your life as a Head you are on show, and attending functions connected with school. Many Saturdays, even in day schools, may be devoted to alumnae reunions, open days, sporting fixtures and local events at which one must represent the school. Very often a Head may have school functions on four or five nights a week – governors' meetings, parents' association meetings, parent-teacher consultation evenings, concerts, plays, debates, open evenings, development committees, alumnae committees, visits to local prep and feeder school open evenings and such events.

Finding time for yourself, your family and friends is not always easy. Those Heads who are fortunate enough to have a school house provided for them (although living in the midst of your work can be a mixed blessing) may also have a home of their own within relatively easy travelling distance to which they can escape for privacy and total relaxation. This is a very good idea.

If you are obliged to live in the goldfish bowl of a school house or in the centre of your catchment area, then cultivating an air which says: 'I am happy to smile in recognition, but please do not engage me in conversation about your child's schooling while I tend my garden, do my shopping, fill my car with petrol…' is undoubtedly an asset. Certainly it is important to go away for holidays and to try not to think about school while you are away – often not a simple task! The advent of email, mobile phones and electronic devices, which allow you to log on to your desktop or be contacted anytime, anywhere, has exacerbated this problem. Strength of resolve is needed to ensure that we are not in work-mode 24/7 and 52 weeks of the year.

Sharing responsibilities with your senior management team and learning the art of delegation are important if you are to have personal space and time. If your school play is performed for four nights do you, as Head, really have to attend all four? If, however, you have been in the habit of doing so and then decide not to, be careful how you manage people's expectations.

Going out and making presentations at feeder schools can be very good experience for your leadership team, but be very clear as to whether it is an event where Heads themselves are expected or not. The Head's presence is not essential at every function, and if that is clearly understood by the school community, take the opportunity to do something else. As has been written in other chapters, shared school leadership is usually more effective than autocracy.

Most Heads are a far cry from the 'me first' attitude which currently seems to be endemic in much of the population. Instead they tend to epitomise altruism. Maintaining personal interests outside school is not being self-centred, but rather keeping a healthy balance. Some Heads are enthusiastic about sports, as participants or spectators; others write, garden, ride motorcycles, walk, watch birds, play music, visit the theatre and concerts. Such interests come in many guises, what matters is that the activities are relaxing, enjoyable and dispel thoughts and concerns about school, even if only for a short time.

Personally, one of the most relaxing things I undertake is gardening: I am not a knowledgeable or gifted gardener, but a very philosophical one. I plant things; sometimes they grow, sometimes they don't; sometimes my fruit and vegetables flourish and I enjoy picking and eating them, sometimes the insects or birds get to them first. No one is calling me to account or putting me in a league table, I am just pottering! I have also kept alive my passion for the classics: I am still involved in various classical organisations and attend or even deliver lectures and try to keep abreast of developments. In this way, I have many friends who are classicists who know me as just another classicist and not as a Head.

Defining your working day is also essential. Some Heads are at their desks very early each morning; others remain in their studies until very late at night; some burn the candle at both ends. Some Heads work long hours at their desk, but rarely take work home; others leave the school building at a reasonable hour, but continue working in their office at home every evening and weekend. Ask yourself: when are you at your best? When is the time that you feel most creative and can think through issues, plan and write? How does this match with the times when you need to be involved in other activities at the school, in meetings, available for pupils, staff and parents or teaching?

Working long hours just for the sake of it is not an effective use of your time or energy, and it can be very detrimental, both to your physical health and your ability to make good decisions. Yes, there may be times when extra hours are needed, but this should be the exception, not the rule, and there is absolutely no point in trying to work when you are too tired to operate effectively. Allowing yourself time to think strategically, to see the big picture, and reflect on how well things are working and how they might be improved is vital. Try to build this time into your life and into your working time not your personal time. If you genuinely think best and most creatively in the bath, then make sure that you build additional long soaks in the bath into your schedule!

It is undeniable that Headship is a stressful role. Heads spend much of their time giving support to others, listening and advising. They act much like a traditional parish priest: people bring their problems to them, sometimes for advice, sometimes just to share and relieve the burden. It might be a member of staff, teaching or non-teaching, worried about ageing parents, wayward children, health problems or marital difficulties. It might be a parent with any of these same problems, or a pupil who is unhappy at home or at school. You may be expected just to listen, to help the person by allowing them to talk about how he/she is feeling, or you may be asked for specific advice. Whichever happens you have acquired another set of confidential information which you probably cannot divulge and which somehow you need to lay to rest.

To whom can Heads talk and with whom can they share their worries? It is rarely a good idea to use your partner or family as the recipient of all your school problems and anxieties, as the result may be growing irritation and resentment. Some Heads have very close and open relationships with their Chairman of governors; many more have a network of other Heads to whom they can turn for advice, support and friendship. Do you have another Head or ex-Head whom you can contact for advice or arrange to meet at short notice? It is certainly worth nurturing such a relationship and it may well be a mutually beneficial arrangement.

Heads spend much time 'giving out' to a wide variety of audiences; making presentations to potential parents, current parents, staff, pupils or governors; leading an assembly or staff meeting. But how do we recharge our batteries? Who or what enables us to be refreshed? For many of us it will be our pupils and staff: watching them develop and achieve and sharing their pleasure in success. Whenever staff or pupils do something well we thank them, congratulate them, write cards and notes – but who does the same for us as Heads?

When things go well in a school, the Head may be praised, but will also take care to recognise the efforts of others. When things go wrong in a school, it is most often the Head who is blamed, who has to accept responsibility and whose future may be called into question. Heads can be dismissed, indeed asked to clear their desks without notice, relatively easily in comparison with any other staff. Maintaining very open and honest relationships with governors is essential, as we have seen elsewhere in this publication, and can help to reduce stress.

Being fit and healthy, both physically and mentally, will certainly enable you to cope more easily with the demands of Headship. Looking after yourself is important. Take time to 'listen to' your body and make sure that you remain in the best health you can. Not only will you be better able to do your job, but also to enjoy your personal life and your retirement. None of us is bionic or superhuman; we cannot do everything which people would wish us to and we must not be afraid to say so.

As I have got older I have realised that making journeys to meetings in London involving a combination of walking, a train and several changes of tube is not conducive to my sangfroid, or best use of my time. For a straightforward journey public transport is good – but for a more complex one, I no longer hesitate to order a cab. However, I have not yet succumbed to the advice given to me at a new Heads' induction course by an experienced London Head, who recommended that one treated oneself to a bottle of champagne every Friday!

The key to maintaining a sensible balance between your personal and work life is to know yourself really well, to be honest about your strengths and weaknesses and about what makes you happy. You need to have a very strong sense of who you are as a person and be confident about yourself. Do not be afraid to say "no", nor to make time for yourself, your family and your friends.

Remember that the more focused you become on the school, the narrower your interests and the more restricted your personal life, the more you will lose your sense of proportion and become myopic and obsessive about school issues. We all have to be in 'Head role' for much of our lives: this is what is expected by our parents, pupils, staff and governors. However, we need to make sure that when we play this role, we are not too far away from our true identity and that we do not neglect those with whom we are able to be completely relaxed and to be ourselves.

And, however young you are, don't forget that one day you will no longer be a Head and that you should make sure that you are well prepared for an interesting and stimulating life of fun and friendship in retirement, leaving behind a happy and successful school.

Chapter 16

Appraisal

Keith Dawson

Cards on the table. I am convinced that appraisal is essential to the well-being and effectiveness of individuals and of schools, and that it should be an integral part of leadership, management and forward planning. If you find this a statement of the obvious, excellent; if not, it's time you did.

The debate about appraisal in schools has lasted almost as long as the unending one about curriculum and examinations for 14-19 year-olds, which has been with us (God help us) since the late 1960s. Although there seems little chance of a coherent solution to the mess at 14-19, some progress has been made over appraisal and related issues. This has hardly been a Damascene conversion; rather a slow realisation that, far from being a threat from management (whoever they may be), appraisal is a *right* of individuals, not least of Heads, that schools have a responsibility to provide.

I first became involved in appraisal in the late 1970s under Tim Brighouse, that great Pied Piper in Oxfordshire, where it worked well. From the start it was *Appraisal for Professional Development*, concerned with the needs both of the individual teacher and of the school, and it was entirely separate from pay or disciplinary procedures. At that time Heads were not formally appraised (to their loss), but they were subjected to rigorous and usually encouraging scrutiny when they presented their school's four-year plan at County Hall.

This was an interesting early link between overall planning and individual appraisal. The development of individuals and the school went hand-in-hand naturally, and usually easily. The point of appraisal was clear and its benefits apparent. Unfortunately, the avalanche of initiatives dumped on schools by the Thatcher governments in the 1980s obliterated that phase of appraisal.

Since the turn of the century, performance review has become an established feature in the public sector. This has come about as part of the largely successful drive to improve leadership and management, and it has helped to take schools forward. A great strength is that it is closely linked to a school's development plan – but, perhaps inevitably, it suffers from the rigidities of all centrally directed systems. It imposes a narrow notion of performance, and is explicitly linked to pay incentives.

Even so, the annual review of Headteachers in state schools has good features. As a nominated governor at our village school in Devon (115 pupils, 4.5 teachers) I took part in reviews of the Head, working with another governor and a registered adviser from a different LEA. The whole process was remarkably thorough and professional. The Head welcomed having time devoted entirely to her work and her aspirations for the school, and we reached agreed targets for her, linked to the school's development plan. She felt supported and better understood. The main feature missing in the framework imposed on us by central government was any opportunity to discuss or help the Head's personal needs and aspirations.

Similar development in independent schools has been patchy. Until quite recently, many in our schools have been unwilling to accept the need for systematic management and development planning. Strong defence of freedom for the individual teacher and a healthy distaste for excessive bureaucracy meant that many schools chose to behave as though they were loose collections of individuals and informal groups. This left them unprepared to meet increasing demands from central government, from the challenges of rapid social change, and of a more volatile and competitive market place.

Traditional attitudes have been changing in last ten years. The leadership of HMC, GSA, and more recently ISC, has been influential in curriculum development, in training provision and in rigorous school inspection through ISI. An incidental benefit of inspection has been the priceless opportunity for professional training and development offered to Heads and senior staff, working as inspectors.

Inspection requires schools to examine themselves, using a comprehensive framework that emphasises good governance, leadership and management. As a result, governors are more engaged, leadership and management are stronger, and noticeable progress is beginning to be made among the middle layer of school staff.

Some independent schools now have effective systems of appraisal, but many still do not. In my experience, schemes often simply pay lip service to the process, failing to link appraisal to the needs or plans of school or department and, crucially, failing to maintain momentum or check progress. Very few include the non-teaching staff – and what does that imply?

Effective appraisal and review should assist the school's aims and objectives, improve performance and support the needs of individuals, teachers and support staff alike. It should ensure that necessary training and professional development is provided. When it works well, appraisal increases confidence and morale and it encourages a sense of common purpose.

Schools have usually first overcome their fear or distaste of appraisal by opting for a peer or buddy system where the person to be appraised is free to choose their appraiser. This will probably be a reassuring and affirming experience concentrating on the appraisee's achievements and personal needs. Necessary and valuable as this is, such appraisal is unlikely to grasp nettles, to measure performance or to set targets for improvement. Moreover, because it isn't linked to a chain of responsibility it will be an event in isolation, unlikely to contribute to the overall good of the school.

Experience suggests that a better system is one that combines a short annual or biennial performance review and target setting, with a more extended event every three or four years when the emphasis is on the personal needs and aspirations of the individual. The idea of performance review has caused unease but there is no good reason why it should. On the contrary, we all need to have our good work and achievements recognised and praised, and a review is an ideal opportunity to do this.

Where things need to be improved by the individual, or by the head of department or the school, it is surely better to deal with this openly rather than to leave it buried and allowed to fester or deteriorate. We are all accountable and a well-ordered appraisal system provides a proper way of making this happen.

In performance review the appraiser should be the line manager. For teachers this will be the head of department, who will receive comment as appropriate from pastoral and other staff. For non-teaching staff, responsibility will lie with their section heads. The Head, or another member of the senior team, appraises the heads of departments and heads of non-teaching sections. This can be quite natural where, as at Bristol, each member of the senior team is given oversight of a group of subjects. The Head carries out the performance review of the senior team and the Head's own performance review is handled either by the Chairman of governors or by two or three other governors nominated by the Chairman. This chain of responsibility helps to integrate the appraisal system with the overall organisation and the development planning of the school, and should foster a sense of common purpose.

The line manager will normally also be responsible for the longer, more personal appraisals, though there could be circumstances when someone else would be more suitable. For the Head, and also for deputies, there is a strong case for bringing in an experienced person from beyond the school who will have a fresh perspective and a dispassionate ear.

Some boards of governors remain diffident about appraising their Head and are unwilling to stray onto the holy ground of the Head's educational expertise (though the growth of governors' education committees is slowly demystifying this). Others, eager for rigorous performance review, seek to inject a whiff of what they are pleased to call 'the real world', by using appraisal models from industry, commerce or the armed forces. There is something to be learned from these models but schools need a process adapted to their peculiar nature.

By now, considerable experience has accumulated of appraising

Heads and it has been thought useful to draw common threads and best practice together, without imposing a rigid pattern from the centre. GSA was the first association to set down guidelines, and their emphasis is on performance review. HMC introduced its own guidance in 2006. It is less prescriptive, leaving it open to individual schools to decide whether or not to introduce formal appraisal systems – but it recommends that they *should* be introduced, and that 'Heads should be formally appraised every three to four years with a performance review at a halfway point'. Both Associations maintain, for the information of governing bodies and others, informal lists of retired (and some current) Heads who do appraisals.

For more than ten years, I have been appraising Heads and deputies in independent and state schools, primary, prep and secondary, mixed and single-sex, boarding and day. They have almost always told me that they found the experience enjoyable, revitalising and useful, both for them and for their school. On the very rare occasions when problems have arisen it has always been because the Chairman or the Head, or both, have sought to use the appraisal to promote a hidden agenda – something to be avoided at all costs. I have enjoyed being able to work independently and to adapt my approach to the needs of individual schools and their Heads, but my general approach is broadly in line with the recommendations already described.

The most precious aspect of an external appraisal is that it gives the Head the undivided time and attention of a neutral expert with no vested interest in the school. This allows a free-ranging discussion of his or her work, successes, problems and needs in what is a uniquely isolated and often a lonely job. In some ways it is also a review of the school; a mini-inspection that can serve a broader purpose than personal appraisal.

Heads tend to be very critical of their own performance and it is rare for them to be on sufficiently open terms with governors or senior colleagues to have an entirely candid discussion with them – certainly not one that would not carry its own baggage. Assessment of their performance over the past three or four years by a dispassionate professional, outside the framework of the school, can encourage the subject to be frank and open in a way that would not be possible otherwise.

Heads are usually clear about what needs improving, and they welcome the opportunity to discuss issues, and perhaps unburden themselves, with someone from outside. Strengths and weaknesses can be confirmed or redefined and ways forward identified. Almost invariably, the appraisal provides an opportunity for the Chairman to praise the Head on the basis of an objective report. The Head will give a lead by undergoing a known, rigorous process and gain added respect and credibility in the Common Room.

In a fully developed system, appraisal will come at regular intervals, but it is especially useful at particular stages. A newish Head should welcome the opportunity two or three years into the job, when there has been time to become established and to have set a course. Established Heads, six to eight years in, can benefit from a fresh look at their work before everything gets too set. Some find it helpful to link their appraisal with preparation a year or two ahead of an inspection or with development planning as a result of an inspection report. Several Heads I have worked with have found the experience helpful as a preparation for retirement in three to four years' time.

This is how I go about it. There is usually a telephone call, either from the Head himself or from a Governor, asking me to appraise. It is essential to agree the terms of trade from the outset, including the time-scale, the stages of the appraisal, who will organise my visits and the nature of the report. I have already mentioned the importance of there being no hidden agendas – the governors' or the Head's. If they exist, they cannot be allowed to drive the process, which must be as objective and impartial as possible. It's best to agree the fee and expenses at this early stage. The HMC guidance includes helpful recommendations and suggests that preparation, time in school and report writing could take up to seven days. I usually find five days sufficient.

Sometimes it is suggested that I might work together with a governor. This can be successful but I prefer to preserve my independence and act alone. However, it is important to keep the Chairman fully informed of what I am doing, and to discuss the project fully at an early stage. I establish whether the governors wish any particular aspects to be included. I make sure the Chairman is fully informed about whom I shall be meeting. I usually meet the Chairman before or soon after beginning my visit and I telephone immediately afterwards to give a brief summary of what will be in my report.

I seek agreement that the report will be confidential to the Head and the Chairman, who alone receive copies. This allows me to write more openly and frankly than would be possible in a more public document. It is for the Head and Chairman to agree between them how the appraisal will be reported to the governing body, and what action will be taken on the targets or recommendations.

If I don't already know the school I usually make a preliminary visit to be shown round, sense the atmosphere and to see the Head in action informally, walking around the school with him, and perhaps joining an assembly and sitting in on a meeting. I ask for written information to work on, a month or so before my visit. The prospectus, magazine, latest inspection report, development plan, management tree and perhaps a recent Head's report to governors all help. These days the school's web site is often a great source of information and a feel for its ethos.

Most appraisers send a questionnaire to staff and other individuals, seeking comment on the Head's qualities, style, achievements, management and communications. I have not done this routinely. It is a considerable undertaking for the school, and can be daunting for the Head, but it can provide initial impressions and help the appraiser to prepare for face-to-face interviews.

I *do* send the Head a questionnaire to complete well ahead of my visit. This ensures that essential areas are covered, including the present condition of the school and forward planning; achievements and frustrations in the past five years (personal and for the school); relationships and communications; administration and use of time; future aims and objectives for the school and for the Head. He is free to add comments that go beyond the questions. This all gives me useful pointers for my interviews with staff and discussion with the Head.

In preparation for the main appraisal meeting, I spend two days interviewing a wide range of people in the school, usually individually, for about half-an-hour each. The Chairman of governors will have briefed me already but it is useful to have the perspective of two or three other key governors. Who else to see depends in detail on local circumstances but usually one of the deputies arranges this once the main categories have been agreed. This keeps things open and above board. The list always includes the senior team, including the bursar, and the Heads of any partner school or related prep school.

There will also be a range of heads of departments (some new, some old), key pastoral staff, the chairman of the Common Room, other staff including a group of recent arrivals, the Head's secretary and the Head's spouse if there is one and if willing. I like to meet a group of pupils, usually over lunch (my reason for being in school may be covered by a convenient fiction), and sometimes I meet a group of parents – but preferably not the Parents' Association Committee.

I have no set agenda for the interviews, but I try to gain a clear picture of each person's view of the condition and health of the school, how it has changed in recent years, what impact the Head has had, how they would characterise his or her style of leadership, and how effective management and communications are. I also seek to add to my picture of the Head and his personal needs.

Successful interviews demand the trust of all concerned. The appraiser can help to encourage this but much depends on the working atmosphere in the school. Everything said is unattributed (although it may well be attributable!) and I encourage as much openness as possible. In nearly every case I have found that people speak freely, candidly and helpfully.

The care and thoughtfulness of almost everyone is impressive and often moving. Many, including the forthrightly critical, have a sympathetic sense of the pressures and isolation of the Head. The last question: 'If you were to give one piece of advice to the Head, what would it be?' frequently produces a telling and supportive response and I list these verbatim in the report.

Seeing 25 to 30 or more different people yields a fascinating scatter of impressions and opinions. Penetrating individual judgements are often illuminating, but there is always much common ground and the main conclusions and judgements are usually clear. Some time is needed to absorb and sift the results of 15-20 hours of interviews before my discussion with the Head. Sometimes I go home and return a few days later, but more often we meet for the whole of the last afternoon.

It is essential to hold the meeting in quiet seclusion. The discussion may only last an hour, but it is wise to clear the diary for three. The place should be one where the Head will be most comfortable. I have had appraisal meetings in a company boardroom and in the hall of a livery company, but these august surroundings are not ideal. It could be away from school or in the study but it must be entirely free from interruptions and other business. The Head's Secretary should be in protective mode and mobile phones must be switched off, even by addicts!

The Chairman may wish to join the meeting, but it should be made clear that this meeting is private between the Head and the appraiser, to allow full and open discussion. A meeting of Head, Chairman and appraiser may be useful but it should follow the main appraisal interview, when the main findings are known and there are unlikely to be difficulties or unhelpful surprises.

It will be unusual if what I have to say is not overwhelmingly positive, but most of us develop distorted hearing on such occasions and the bass, negative tones all too easily drown out the soaring treble. However experienced or outwardly serene s/he may be the Head is bound to be anxious, usually the more so the less the need. S/he will also be acutely aware that people from all parts of the school have been having their say, and only an extraordinarily self-confident character will not be on tenterhooks.

The interview must therefore give the Head every opportunity to say what s/he wants. The response to the questionnaire provides a useful framework and the conversation often leads on usefully from there. The judgements of others become part of the ensuing conversation to support or extend the Head's comments. It is rare for an issue to come as a surprise. It is best for the Head to introduce an issue personally, and this may be the first opportunity s/he has had to talk through a knotty problem or a deep frustration. A disinterested appraiser may provide what no one in the school can.

Proper attention must be given to the Head's personal needs. I've only once known an appraisal in which the pressure the Head puts on himself and on his family has not been an issue. Some years ago the management sage Charles Handy concluded that secondary schools were essentially unmanageable – not least because Heads were directly answerable to all and sundry in ways that simply do not happen with company chief executives. Some of this is self-inflicted. Many Heads have over-developed consciences and are too eager to be involved in everything. Many don't delegate (trust?) enough and don't make proper time for their personal lives. A good appraisal can find ways out of the maze.

The interview should have reached agreed conclusions and targets that will be included in the report. I aim to send a draft for comment by the Head about a week later. It is set in the context of the present condition of the school and the Head's experience. There is an account of his or her achievements since appointment, or in the past five years, and of problems or frustrations.

I summarise what I have learned about his qualities and style of leadership and management, his strengths and any significant weaknesses. The advice of senior colleagues usually confirms what has gone before, and I quote it verbatim to keep the impact fresh. The final section summarises his targets for the school and for himself. If we can't agree about any part of the report the Head is free to add personal comments directly to the Chairman, but this very rarely happens.

Appraisal shouldn't be cosy but it should leave the Head and the school feeling positive and better able to face the future. If it has been successful it will help progress and have a key place alongside the development plan and the inspection report.

Afterword

Nigel Richardson

In today's world, the specialist is highly valued – and very well paid – be it in industry, the professions or the media. The generalist tends to be less well regarded. Yet, if there is one thing that comes through from the chapters in this collection of essays about the work of a Head, it is the generalist nature of our work. It would be hard to imagine more varied demands, or a more all-embracing job description, than those which our job implies – educator and curriculum thinker, strategist, marketer, PR expert, budget planner, personnel manager, disciplinarian, marriage guidance counsellor, and so on.

There are some recurring themes in these pages, too. First, the public nature of, and interest in, our role, at a time when education has become a national preoccupation (bordering on obsession), as the UK faces up to the competition posed by both the knowledge economy and global market, and when the national press prints huge numbers of articles about schools every day – all valuably tracked by the ISC daily bulletin.

Secondly, the social and other demands on Heads to provide for society much of what the clergyman and the doctor once provided – and sometimes to be a substitute parent for children in families under huge work and relationships pressures, and advisor to staff whose professional stresses can be very great.

Thirdly, on the need for us Heads to avoid the prone-ness of many people in our profession to be workaholics, and obsessively conscientiousness. To give ourselves time to think strategically, and to relax. To examine our own performance critically, but positively too. And to prepare sensibly for the day when we shall lock the study door for the last time – and maybe even be brave enough to throw all the old teaching notes away…

Schools still tend to be pyramidic in structure and style, with staff and parents seeking out the Head when others might do. Yet this book also reflects the huge growth in management teamwork in recent years – and the need for Heads to trust and develop their deputies. One of the great breakthroughs of the past 25 years in the independent sector has been the emergence of a proper career structure for would-be Heads, as the role of the deputy has increasingly been externally advertised, and as directors of studies have gained greater influence and experience. The great majority of new Heads have now held such a role – although this still perhaps applies more in day schools than boarding schools, where house-mastering experience is so important. Little wonder, therefore, that a number of successful schools are now appointing their own deputy to be Head, when the vacancy arises.

We are very grateful to our writing team, who universally delivered their text on time and in a state which required comparatively little editing. Despite their best efforts, we have not been able to cover everything: for example, we have included only the smallest reference to the sort of disciplinary investigation which can take over the life of even the best organised Head for a week or more. But this publication is planned as the first of a series of publications, and we shall devote a chapter in our next volume (about deputy headship and management team issues) to this theme.

Meanwhile the need to train Heads has never been greater. The average age of the current crop is alarmingly high, and the whole generation of so-called baby-boomer school Heads – born, like me, in the years after World War Two – is now reaching retirement. In the maintained sector, attention is being focused on a serious shortage of would-be successors. The National College for School Leadership talks about fast-tracking would-be members of the next generation of school leaders from the age of 30. There have been calls for more federations of schools led by a single Head – although that is far from straightforward – and for more distributed leadership amongst teams to take pressure off Heads.

The independent sector faces similar challenges – real ones, even if they come in a less acute form. And one particular sentence from a paper prepared by Michael Fullan which appears in a recent report for the DCSF by PricewaterhouseCoopers LLP has gone round in my mind as I read these pages:

> *The success of school leaders should be measured, not in terms of their impact on student achievement seen during their tenure, but rather on how many leaders they have developed and left behind who can go even further than they did.*

(*The Hope for Leadership in the Future* by Michael Fullan, Ontario Institute for Studies in Education, University of Toronto.)

It is our hope that this book will contribute to that process of bringing on the next generation.

NOTES

NOTES

NOTES

Notes

NOTES